MW01043051

# Critical Skills
## for Life and Leadership
### The New Science of Personal and
### Organizational Development

RYAN A. KUETER

Copyright © 2019 Ryan A. Kueter

All rights reserved.

ISBN: 0-578-55690-1
ISBN-13: 978-0-578-55690-1

# CONTENTS

# CONTENTS

# PREFACE

Thank you for reading *Critical Skills for Life and Leadership: The New Science of Personal and Organizational Development*. Modern societies are faced with a multitude of problems, like crime, mismanagement, pollution, or corruption. And mitigating these problems requires more than government interventions that disincentivize harmful behavior. People need to change the way they think and operate. And specifically, Science needs to make progress towards developing the skills required to advance the human intellect.

This book presents, what I believe to be, the most scientific, practical, and interdisciplinary way to study and develop human behavior, the human intellect, and human organizations. This book not only looks at what happens when human development goes wrong, but what needs to happen to make it go right. For example, when people lack certain intellectual skills, the consequence is often predictable and preventable problems. You can see that in occupational roles, where a skills deficit would result in incompetence or malpractice. But it also happens in the course of people's everyday lives where skills deficits cause conflicts, poor decisions, failing relationships, harmful assumptions, unemployment, and even more serious problems, like crime. In fact, life skills programs are often created with the intention of reducing these types of problems.

1

The research presented in this book has many applications, including parenting, management, instruction, and even governmental policy. One such application, which is explored only briefly in this book, is criminal rehabilitation. Arguably, the State owes a duty of care to the public to use an inmate's incarceration as an opportunity to change the inmate's thinking before being released back into the public. That requires overcoming the thinking, or mental disorders, that result in criminal behaviors, in addition to improving the life skills that make those behaviors unnecessary. If such programs could be successful, communities would benefit from reduced incarceration expenses, fewer crimes and arrests, and safer and more satisfied citizens. And ideally, those programs would continue to evolve and become more effective overtime.

The same could be said about education and other types of social problems experienced in communities. By using the methods presented in this book, a Behavioral Scientist could even identify a targeted problem, and create a developmental solution for resolving that problem. Only by observing this cause-and-effect relationship between specific problems, and how skills enable people to resolve those problems, can the researcher further develop those skills to create more desirable outcomes.

The first chapter of this book explores the science of skills development, and how learned abilities have an effect on a person's overall condition, mental health, and outlook on life. The chapters that follow explore how specific intellectual skills, like critical thinking skills, motivational skills, responsibility, stress management, and other skills, enable you to be more effective in performing your life roles.

This book contains many of my own scientific theories and original ideas on subjects, like motivation, mental health, and others, developed during the last couple of decades. The supporting evidence presented in this book comes from a variety of behavioral sciences, rather than a specific school of thought, to create a more complete picture of human behavior and its influences.

My belief is that as you learn more about human development and the skills that enable you to more effectively perform your roles, the more capable you will be in guiding your own development, the development of other people, and maintaining your overall condition. By reading this book, my hope is that you gain the insight and inspiration into creating the life, career, and future you really want.

# CHAPTER I:
# INTRODUCTION

In popular culture, heroes are admired for their extraordinary gifts, powers, and super-human strengths. The audience thrills to heroes on the big-screen as they watch the hero's bold and death-defying acts to risk life and limb, and perform extraordinary feats of courage, to save the person in need. And while that fantastic over-the-top heroism is beyond the capabilities of the average person, people do play out their own mundane forms of heroism in their life roles, as a parent, in their career, or in their service to a cause. Each person has their own unique strengths that make them heroic in the eyes of those who depend on them in their personal lives and careers. And this book is entirely about how to strengthen those abilities to make you more effective in your everyday life.

In this chapter, we look at conditions that are conducive to, or prevent, the development of healthy life skills. People have long sought answers to questions like: What makes a person of good character? Or, what makes a great leader? And this book answers those questions by exploring the development of intellectual skills that enable people to be more effective, not just in their character or leadership, but in all of their life roles.

1
The Science of Human Abilities

Beyond the study of Physiology, like brain anatomy, Neurology, Biochemistry, or Genetics, the science of human behavior largely focuses on different types of abilities, including learned responses (both normal or maladaptive) and skills development. Behavior is comprised of many different types of uniquely defined abilities. And abilities have some interesting properties that make them perfect for scientific study.

To start with, you can test for an ability, which enables you to observe and measure it. And if an ability can be measured, it may be possible to further develop it. Abilities also have a profound influence on the way people think and develop, in addition to decision-making, mental health, and all aspects of performance. This book not only looks at how to study various skills or abilities, but how to develop them for the purpose of resolving specific problems of living, like performing life roles or achieving goals.

A *skill* is an ability that enables you to operate, solve problems, achieve goals, and more effectively perform roles. Skills are like mind muscles that grow stronger or weaker depending on use or disuse. And skills, like social skills, parenting skills, or management skills, enable you to more effectively create the outcomes you really want. For example, a Tennis player may practice to overcome certain weaknesses and become a stronger player, to improve one's chances of winning.

My belief is that one of the technologies of the human sciences involves how to use Science to further develop healthy life skills to improve people's lives. Skills are like the features and functionality of the human machine that can be further enhanced, or debugged, to improve how people think, operate, and perform their roles. In fact, as people age, they are forced to adapt to new environments and learn new tasks, perform new jobs, and follow new rules. This behavioral adaptation is a process of developing skills in response to environmental challenges to more effectively perform tasks, perform roles, and achieve goals.

This book connects the dots between human abilities that make people more effective in their life roles, and how those abilities solve problems, which could be called the *skills theory of social problems*. Your basic learned abilities provide you with the means to interact with the world around you. And those learned abilities can be improved by developing specific skills, like thinking skills, communication skills, and other types of skills that make you more effective in your everyday life.

The whole purpose of studying behavior and mental processes as learned abilities is that, not only can you more effectively isolate and study those abilities, you can develop specific abilities to produce a wanted outcome. For example, if you wanted to develop healthier behaviors and live a healthier lifestyle, you need to develop specific healthy life skills, like food preparation, or knowing what foods to eat. Without those skills, living a healthier lifestyle is not possible.

This, I believe, is the true science of human behavior and the mind. Just as a Physicist views an object as consisting of atomic particles, or the Earth's atmosphere as consisting of layers of gasses, the Behavioral Scientist views behavior and mental processes as consisting of a collection of learned abilities that can be isolated and studied to enable people to be more effective in their daily lives. Training on certain types of intellectual skills not only improves the social dynamics within personal relationships and in human organizations, it improves a person's efficacy and dependability as a decisionmaker. When people are not trained on certain critical skills, the consequence is usually a variety of preventable problems. At worst, you end up with people who lack those critical skills in positions where they make risky and highly impactful decisions that produce a variety of predictable and preventable problems.

In industry, skills are the human factors of success and failure. In business, for example, the factors of production normally include things, like time, labor, or materials, necessary to produce a good or service. But the human factors presented in this book may be more critical to determining the success or failure of a person or organization, than any other factor considered in economic models.

In this book, think of a factor as anything that influences an end result. For example, in grade school, you may have learned about math functions, like (y) equals a function with (x) provided as a parameter. Each (x) inputted into the function changes the value of (y). So, if (y) is a cheesecake, and each (x) is a specific amount of an ingredient inputted into the function, then as you change each (x-ingredient), the flavor of the (y-cheesecake) changes correspondingly.

In business, some of those factors include professional competencies, which can certainly improve operational efficiencies, lower costs, and make organizations more effective. But this book explores a different set of human factors that include intellectual skills, like critical thinking skills, motivational skills, personal skills, and so many others. No matter how much you develop your professional skillset, without certain core intellectual skills, you are less able to perform those roles, and more likely to experience other negative consequences that influence your success.

Your progress, in terms of learning how to perform your roles, entirely depends on the development of your skillsets. At every stage of life, you are either learning new abilities as a result of engagement and effort, or losing old abilities as a result of forgetting or age-related conditions. When an infant learns to speak, those communication skills will enable the child to solve problems related to communication throughout life. At a later age, when a child learns to read or type, those skills solve problems related to academic learning and certain types of productivity. And at some point, young adults hopefully learn the skills that enable them to be responsible adults. Naturally, not all people learn these skills equally. But by studying these learned abilities, researchers are able to understand the skills required to perform life roles so that people can become better parents, better managers, better instructors, or better leaders, and understand how skills deficits prevent people from performing their roles responsibly.

Practitioners of this new science apply knowledge to developing the skills necessary for people and organizations to be successful. We have seen how people, as individuals, benefit from this research by learning how to effectively and confidently perform life roles. But this research could also be applied to organizations, to understand whether the organization has the abilities to operate effectively and profitably. And, specifically, it looks at whether members have the skillsets to perform their roles effectively, and the negative consequences of lacking those skills, in terms of inefficiencies, lost revenues, negligence, or faulty practices. A program engineer could, then, use techniques to develop workforce training programs for the development of those organizational abilities.

Learned abilities also have many psychological effects on thinking, behavior, and life choices. They tend to expand, or limit, your potential, and influence how you respond to difficulties, what you think about yourself, the types of goals you pursue, and your successes. If you enjoy challenging your abilities, you may see a difficult problem as an opportunity to learn, develop, and grow stronger. But if you see a difficult problem as beyond your abilities, you may try to avoid it.

B. F. Skinner once observed how a tennis player practices until he achieves a certain level of consistency in his game. And that frequent reinforcement "builds faith" in his abilities, and builds confidence in his success.[55] Alfred Adler gave another example of how a marathon runner who does not "trust himself" to hurdle an obstacle, tries to avoid it.[1] And in later sections of this chapter, we look at the work of Psychologists, like Carol Dweck, Martin Seligman, and others, who have contributed to the research about how human abilities influence the way people think.

This book also looks at the many different factors involve with human development. Genetics, for instance, can certainly give you an advantage in specific roles, like height in basketball, physical attraction in modelling, or vocal abilities in music. But biology, alone, does not completely determine human ability. In fact, you have more control, and more choice, over the development of your skills than anything else in your life. If you have a choice of becoming wealthy by luck or skill, you would want to choose skill because you have more control over your skills development than you do over luck or chance.

## 2
## The Value of Skills

Skills are valuable for many reasons. First of all, skills can influence your self-esteem. As you develop your skills, you have more to contribute, more to offer, and people may come to depend on you. When skills have monetary exchange value, they are called *human capital*. For example, when people have a problem they do not know how to fix, like a broken appliance, they usually hire an expert to fix it. Or when an organization hires a new worker, the collection of skills that worker brings to the job usually solves some problem in the organization. People are willing to pay for good solutions to their problems, so they do not have to spend their valuable time and energy learning from mistakes and figuring it out themselves. In this respect, accumulating human capital can make you more confident in your ability to earn a living and financially support yourself, which can lead to other psychological and social benefits.

Skills add a significant amount of economic value because they improve decision-making and prevent negative consequences. For example, suppose you are told your Brain Surgeon does not have any formal education or surgical skills. Can you be absolutely certain that you will not die, or become paralyzed, during surgery? Or suppose a structural engineer designs a building without any formal training or design skills. Can you be certain that the building will not sink into the ground, catch on fire, and kill everyone inside? Managers of hospitals and engineering firms are incentivized, if not legally then financially incentivized, to hire qualified professionals because the consequences of not doing so could be catastrophic. These simple truths may appear to be obvious, to many people. But you will find medical doctors and building engineers in some countries that do not see the same value in those skills. And what is less obvious is the value that skills add to other life roles.

In business, a lack of certain types of management skills can cause a decline in productivity, employee turnover, conflict that reduces cooperation, a perception of unfairness, and a decline in sales. Some examples of management skills include the ability to create a fair workplace, hire and promote qualified workers, hold workers accountable, give credit where credit is due, and monitor the quality of production without micromanaging. This brief list may appear to have been created in a sudden brainstorm, as if I woke up one night in a cold sweat and wrote it on a piece of paper. But this list was actually created from material in this book, as a result of researching skills, and understanding the negative operational and financial impact that skills deficits can have on an organization. Sadly, while many of these skills deficits could completely ruin an organization, they are often not taught in the School of Business at Universities.

On the topic of parenting, effective parenting skills can improve outcomes for both the parents and children. If you are a parent, you want to help your child to develop the abilities necessary to be a successful and independent adult. And you can do that by encouraging the child to take on difficult, but achievable, tasks that involve social interaction, learning, or problem solving, which will improve the child's ability to confront and take on similar challenges in the future. As the child builds the self-confidence necessary to take-on other types of challenges, that child is more likely to mature into a healthy and independent adult.

3
Life Roles

*Life roles* include any role you perform in life. For example, you may be an employee, a manager, a business owner, or a leader. And each of those roles is defined by a different set of abilities and a different skillset. And further developing those skills can enable you to be more effective and successful in performing those roles. If you want to develop those abilities today, your options include role modelling, character development, education, and self-help, some of which are more effective than others for improving your performance.

Role modelling can be instrumental in helping you learn the skills required to perform a role. That is especially true if you have a great role model. But role modelling, alone, has obvious limitations, especially when your role model is a bad example. A more effective approach may involve identifying the skillset required to perform a role, and encouraging the development of those skills. Of course, you could simply ask a person who was successful in a role for advice. And that person may be able to provide unscientific guidance on developing that role, while not understanding the underlying reasons one's approach worked. But Science may also be able to provide us with a better understanding of what is proven to work from case studies and other forms of research.

Character development can also be instrumental in helping you develop the skills for performing a life role. *Character* is a creative expression of the self that consists of a unique collection of personal qualities, mannerisms, and capabilities that are characteristic of who you are. And because of this, character tends to be highly subjective and a matter of opinion. But character can also be improved by developing intellectual skills, like decision-making skills. In movies and in television shows, characters are often exaggerated into superheroes or evil villains, depending on their actions and how they are characterized. But in real-life, your character is hopefully less pretentious and overly dramatic than the fictional characters you see in the movies.

Character can be influential on whether a person is liked or disliked. When considering whether a person is suitable for a role as a spouse or an employee, the focus is often on character because of the appearance that the person's character brings to the role. For example, if a hiring manager is choosing between two candidates for a corporate management position, and one candidate is dressed in dirty street clothes while the other has a professional appearance, the hiring manager may prefer the person with the professional appearance because of the appearance that person brings to the role.

Character development can be instrumental in managing your development, productivity, and stress by guiding the development of skills that are characteristic of who you aspire to be. For instance, developing the ability to care for other people, be a problem solver, have a strong work ethic, create a track record of success, or be an expert in your career. During times of distress, seeing yourself as a "rational person," or a "strong person," or not being an angry person, may help you maintain self-control and manage stress by staying in character. If you have qualities that are uncharacteristic of who you are, maybe anger issues or drinking, staying in character may help you avoid those tendencies. In fact, the reason people sometimes lie is to hide character flaws (i.e., qualities that are uncharacteristic of how the person wants to be perceived), like a drug addiction.

But character can also be deceptive because it can be entirely forged out of lies. And that is exactly what con-artists, or confidence artists, do when trying to convince unsuspecting people to hand over their money for illicit purposes. Even when people are not committing crimes, they will lie about their accomplishments or level of expertise. In business, it's not uncommon to find someone who pretentiously gives the appearance and mannerism of sophistication or authority, or strives to be likeable by having a charming personality, but lacks the skills to perform the role that one was hired for.

Life goals, like creating a family, or pursuing a career, can also be instrumental in guiding your development and shaping who you want to be as they give you a cause, or calling, to pursue. Human behavior is highly goal-oriented. You are biologically motivated to pursue goals for satiation, safety, self-protection, and excretion. You also have future goals that require the ability to recognize, and make predictions about, future outcomes. Those goals are more complex and require thinking, planning, and strategy, and depend on the development of intellectual abilities. As a member of a human society, you are required to follow social rules to get what you want or face negative consequences. For example, in the United States, you are required to pay for food instead of stealing it. By following these socially prescribed rules of behavior, you are able to gain the trust necessary to develop the personal relationships to achieve your goals.

Life goals also help you to focus your energy. People who are not pursuing life goals are often directionless, and may not know what to do. In a later chapter on motivation, we look at Dr. Edwin Locke's Goals Setting Theory and how goal-setting can be motivational because it provides a person with a course of action. Without clear goals and a plan of action, it's difficult to know how to proceed, what activities to engage in, and you may spend your time idly doing nothing.

4
Mindsets

In her book *Mindset: The New Psychology of Success*, Carol Dweck presents two divergent viewpoints: 1) the fixed mindset, which views human intelligence as fixed and limited, and incapable of further growth or development; and 2) the growth mindset, which views human abilities as having the potential to grow and develop.[20]

According to Dweck, a person with a fixed mindset typically believes that intelligence and talent are fixed traits that people are born with. In other words, a person's intelligence does not change or improve during the course of one's life. People who are born smart do not have to work as hard, intellectually, as a person who was not born smart. So, a person with a fixed mindset may have a greater fear of failure and rejection as a result of not being smart enough, and may use tactics to avoid appearing unintelligent. A fixed mindset person may avoid challenging or difficult problems that appear beyond one's capabilities, to avoid the embarrassment of failure. Or a fixed mindset person may lie to coverup shortcomings in one's abilities, or put on a pretentious façade to appear smart, or cheat to get ahead. To a person with a fixed mindset, these strategies seem necessary to get ahead, since one's intelligence is fixed and unchanging, and one is at a disadvantage in comparison to smarter people.

To a person with a growth mindset, on the other hand, intelligence and talent can be changed and improved with effort and persistence. To a person with a growth mindset, failure does not mean that one is not smart enough, but rather not enough time and effort was put into achieving the end result. Instead of fearing failure, a person with a growth mindset may welcome difficult challenges to one's abilities that provide the opportunity to develop in new ways, grow stronger, and improve when faced with similar challenges. A person with a growth mindset may also be more resilient, and capable of overcoming rejection and failure, and more willing to overcome personal limitations.

Dweck points out instances in which these divergent mindsets influence life decisions and personal development. For instance, a student with a fixed mindset may be discouraged from learning, may drop out of a challenging academic course, and may avoid it or give-up as a result of not being smart enough. A student with a growth mindset, on the other hand, may view the same subject as a worthy challenge that only becomes difficult as a result of not studying.

Fixed and growth mindsets also influence how people treat other people. An instructor with a fixed mindset may only help students who appear to be smart enough, and give-up on students who are not. Parents who have a fixed mindset toward their children may only help those who appear to have potential. Or in the business world, a fixed mindset manager may look for workers who are already smart and perform at a high level on the first day, rather than training-up and developing talent within. That, of course, limits the talent the organization has to draw from and leads to excuses about why the company cannot be more successful. The growth mindset manager is more likely to overlook imperfections and focus on developing talent. By viewing people as capable of being coached, trained, and improved overtime, the manager is able to take more responsibility for the success of the organization, and appreciate the value of the workforce, rather than creating excuses for skills failures and blaming it on the labor market.

5

Escape from Helplessness

Another way that human abilities have a profound influence on decision-making is when a lack of ability leads to a feeling of helplessness. During the 1960's at the University of Pennsylvania, Psychologists Martin Seligman and Steven Maier conducted an experiment to study the behavior of two groups of dogs: An escape group and a no-escape group. The escape group consisted of dogs that were exposed to electric shocks, which the dogs had the option of terminating by pressing a panel. The no-escape group consisted of dogs that were exposed to electric shocks they were not able to escape, or control in any way. When a dog from the escape group was put into a shuttle box, which is a large box divided into two compartments, and an electric current was supplied to the floor of the dog's compartment, the dog learned to jump over the dividing partition into the other compartment to escape the shock. But when dogs from the no-escape group were put into the shuttle box and were exposed to the electric shock, they did not try to escape, even when escape was possible.

The conclusion that Seligman and Maier arrived at was that, because the dogs in the escape group learned that their actions could stop the shocks, they learned to take action and jump over the partition into the other compartment. But the dogs in the no-escape group learned that their actions could not stop the shocks, so they did not try to escape and, instead, developed learned helplessness. Seligman went on to study the role of learned helplessness in depression in people.[28] And in his most recent book, *The Hope Circuit: A Psychologist's Journey from Helplessness to Optimism*,[54] Seligman said that during those early days, no dogs were harmed, the dogs were cured of learned helplessness before being released and, during the last forty years, he has not performed any experiments on animals.

In the human world, we could see how learned helplessness could have a number of potential causes. When a person is in a miserable situation and perceives a lack of control over life, that person may be less likely to do anything about it and may become depressed. For example, a child who is unable to escape the daily mistreatment of an abusive parent may be likely to accept the mistreatment. Or when a person is trapped in an unsatisfying job or a miserable relationship, and feels helpless to do anything about it, the person is more likely to give up and accept a miserable state of affairs. When a person stops trying as a result of feeling helpless, it is a symptom of depression.

My own conclusion about Seligman and Maier's research, and from my own life experiences with a colleague who overcame a depressive episode twenty years ago, is that learned helplessness may also be attributed to a lack of confidence in one's abilities to overcome significant difficulties. And that could lead to despair and giving up. If my hunch is correct, then, in theory, a person may gradually overcome the perception of helplessness by setting goals for one's development and pursuing those goals, so long as that development is possible.

In theory, further developing social or occupational skills, and increasing confidence in the ability to overcome certain problems, can enable a person to overcome the symptoms of depression. But it's a process that takes time, since skills development takes time. Rather than being a quick and immediate solution, like a medication, skills development and improving self-confidence takes months, if not years. But, unlike medication, which sometimes only treats the symptoms of a disorder, skills development treats the root causes related to why a person feels helpless and depressed. People who have developed that inner flame of self-confidence, may be more mentally prepared to take-on the difficulties of life, and may be less likely to despair and give-up.

6

The Principle of Gradual Improvement

At the core of personal development is the *Principle of Gradual Improvement*, which suggests that the more you work to overcome the limitations of an ability, the stronger that ability becomes. Intuitively, you could say: The more you do something, the better you get. But that is true, only to a diminishing extent. The more you practice, reflect on, and finetune an ability, the stronger that ability becomes. For example, the more times you practice remembering something, the stronger that memory becomes, which improves your fitness in performing that task. Or, the more conversations you have, the more questions you think of and the more topics you talk about. And this principle can be applied to performing just about any task or life role.

K. Anders Ericsson, who has spent more than 30 years researching expertise, explains in his book *Peak: Secrets from the New Science of Expertise* that hard work and deliberate practice may be more responsible for talent and expertise, than innate gifts or job experience. He makes the point that just because someone has performed a task, repeatedly, for many years does not make that person better overtime.[22] An amateur tennis player, he explained, may become good enough to play against other players. But his skills eventually plateau and stop improving. In fact, his skills may even decline as a result of forgetting. The root of the problem, he says, is that people get comfortable in their occupational roles, develop automated routines, and stop learning and developing in new ways, especially when they are not required.

What influences the development of expertise the most, according to Ericsson's research, is the amount of work put into improving that expertise. And, specifically, people make the most progress when they are laser-focused on strengthening weak abilities. But to do that, you need to know where your weaknesses are.

In my experience, one of the best ways to identify your weaknesses is by seeking expert guidance, which can accelerate the learning process and rapidly improve your skills. For instance, a skill that would take you a year to develop as a result of being self-taught, from trail-and-error, and from learning from mistakes, may only take you a week or a month to develop under the guidance of an expert who has already learned from those mistakes and can provide you with beneficial feedback.

If you want to really develop your skills, according to Ericsson, then perform a task that requires more effort and causes you to make mistakes. When you learn something new, you are forced to face your lack of knowledge and make mistakes, which forces your brain to exert extra effort to change and adapt. That gives you the opportunity to recognize weaknesses, learn, and strengthen those abilities with practice and persistence. If you only remain in your comfort zone and perform tasks you are already good at, you will not develop any further in your abilities, and you will not improve, no matter how many years you do it.

# 7
## Behavioral Change

The marketplace is teaming with ideas and advice on how to change your behavior, or develop new habits that make you a more effective person, communicator, or leader. But this section looks at how behavioral change is truly only possible by learning new behaviors, or abilities, that serve as the building blocks for new habits.

A *habit* is a response to routine circumstances that becomes more automatic with repetition. Habits are so automatic that people tend to default back to habits when making life choices, since they require less effort than thinking, predicting, or problem solving. In the *Power of Habit: Why We Do What We Do in Life and Business*, New York Times journalist Charles Duhigg explores the science and applications of habits in a variety of different subjects including neurology, business, marketing, and sports. In the first chapter, he explores the structure of a habit, as identified by MIT researchers, and how habits are triggered by cues.[18] Deciding what to eat for lunch because it's noon time, or deciding to wash hands because they are dirty, are examples of habits triggered by environmental cues. And habits differ by complexity, some having a specific order of multiple steps. But the one thing all habits have in common is that the amount of mental effort required to perform a task decreases as they are repeated, learned, and become more habituated.

Many habits seem to define the way people live. For example, you have dietary consumption habits, habits for hygiene, like brushing teeth, and physical activity habits, that may contribute to a healthy or unhealthy lifestyle. Or you have emotional attitudes in the way you respond to people and circumstances. You have social habits in the way you introduce yourself and whether you are polite. You have purchasing habits in the way you budget and spend your money. You have work habits and devote a certain amount of time to work and practice. You also have work habits on the job, in terms of how you perform a job.

Since habits have such a profound influence on lifestyle choices, the goal of many behavioral change programs focuses on getting rid of old habits, or substituting an old habit with a new habit. The problem with that is that old habits do not die because they are deeply rooted and have established mental connections that remain, even if you wanted them to disappear. In fact, it could take years if not decades for habits to atrophy and be forgotten. And it's much easier to default back to old habits and behavioral patterns that already established and require no effort.

Instead, real behavioral change focuses on learning and developing new skills. Think of developing new skills as planting new flowers in your garden. Your old habits are the weeds or flowers you do not want in your garden. And since you cannot reach into your brain and uproot those old weeds and flowers, the only thing you can do is try to nourish your new flowers and let the old ones die on their own.

New skills provide you with a new method of operating from which new habits will emerge. For example, changing your lifestyle habits is not merely a matter of substituting unhealthy lifestyle habits with healthy lifestyle habits. It requires a learning process of learning about healthy food, healthy ingredients, developing your ability to make healthy meals that are delicious and desirable to eat, and learning how to prepare, or purchase, those foods. That requires a significant investment in time and energy learning about nutrition, long before you can change your daily routine or incorporate it into your diet. If learning these new healthier skills does not take place, you will never change your lifestyle habits. You will never know where to buy the food, how to prepare the food, and it will never be delicious enough. So, you will eventually give up and default back to your old habits.

Behavioral change and, specifically, developing new behavior, comes from developing new skills. And learning a new skill often takes time, as we will see in next section. For example, you may have to think through steps, double-check yourself, ask questions, or learn from mistakes. But after you learn and practice a skill, it becomes increasingly more automatic and habitual.

## 8
## The Learning Curve

The learning curve commonly refers to the amount of time and effort required to learn, or master, a new subject. Even if you have not mastered a subject, you know by the Principle of Gradual Improvement that if you spend more time learning, practicing, and working on a subject, you will gradually improve. And if you spend enough time developing your skills and expertise, you will eventually get over the learning curve.

One of the earliest references to the learning curve comes from the 1880's, from Psychologist Hermann Ebbinghaus, who used it to represent proficiency and the rate at which a person learns a subject. In Hermann's model, the vertical Y-axis represents proficiency and the horizontal X-axis represents the time spent learning. Starting at zero, a person's proficiency and knowledge increases as the amount of time spent learning increases.

During later decades, Theodore P. Wright in his 1936 book Factors Affecting the Cost of Airplanes, borrowed the learning curve concept and applied it to Management Science. Wright's version was different in that it did not focus on expertise but, instead, the rate of production. In Write's model, the vertical Y-axis represents the average time (or labor cost) required to produce a unit of product, and the horizontal X-axis represents the cumulative volume of production. When the cumulative volume of production is at zero, the average time required to produce a unit is high. And the amount of time required to produce each unit decreases with each additional unit produced. For example, suppose you are hired to assemble chairs at a furniture manufacturer. When you assemble your first chair, you have to think through each step, or maybe ask questions, so you do not make a mistake during assembly. As you assemble each additional unit, each step is being sequenced in memory so that the amount of time it takes to produce each additional unit decreases, maybe from 10 minutes to 3 minutes.

These two different versions of the learning curve illustrate two different types of learning. The first represents expertise and knowledge accumulation, and the second represents performance and efficiency gains from repeating a task. The rates at which different people learn will be different for each person. But it may be possible to shorten that learning curve, depending on how a subject is presented. For example, if you provided a Trigonometry student with just enough information required to learn the subject (e.g., concise definitions and simple workflows) the student should be able to get over the learning curve much faster than someone required to read the history of Trigonometry and lengthy technical explanations that would make a relatively simple subject complex and time-consuming. Once the student has gotten over the learning curve, the student can move on to more advanced subjects and attain a higher-level of education.

In recent decades, competing forms of instruction have emerged on the internet, which has dramatically reduced the learning curve by increasing the rate at which people learn and perform work. Back in the 1980's, if you wanted to research a subject and you lived in a small-town in Oklahoma, like I did, you would take a 30-minute commute to the library. If you knew what you were looking for, you would flip through a card catalogue to find where it was located in the library. And if you could not find it, you would go to the most logical section in the library, and look for a publication that closely resembled what you were looking for. If you got lucky and found one, the publication was probably 10 years out-of-date. Today, you can pick up a laptop and research anything in the known universe, attend a college course, get the latest news, and stream entertainment, all at the same time straight to your couch in your living-room.

Textbook writers should strongly consider the instruction methods presented by these new technologies, not just as supplemental material, but as an example of how to present the material. Enormous potential still remains for new technology to not only extend human abilities by enabling people to do things they otherwise would not, but to further develop new human abilities with the assistance of digital tutors, digital coaches, and digital instructors. A future where people walk around with their own army of robot assistants may not be as far off as it may seem.

9

The Confidence Effect

*Self-confidence*, in this book, is defined as confidence in your abilities, which as we have already seen has a profound psychological effect on behavior. Under-confidence, or lacking enough confidence, can prevent a person from being able to solve life problems, which may lead to giving-up. Over-confidence, and having too much confidence, can deceive a person into believing that something is possible when it is not. For example, you may have a high level of confidence in your ability to win the lottery. But that would go against the astronomical odds of winning, unless you figure out a way to defeat the odds, or cheat.

So, to realistically improve your self-confidence, you need to further develop those abilities. A high level of confidence is encouraging, and instills courage in the face of difficulties. A lack of confidence, in contrast, may make you more susceptible to fears, worries, despair, and giving up. And in a later section, we look at how confidence plays a significant role in mental health, in recovering from traumatic events, and when making significant life choices.

Even if a skillset is not fully developed, with a growth mindset you can have confidence in your ability to develop those skills. So long as a challenge to your abilities is realistic and achievable, you may see a difficult problem as an opportunity to learn, develop, and grow stronger. If you see a difficult problem as beyond your abilities, you may see that problem as something that should be avoided. So, self-confidence has a profound effect on your motivation, the types of goals you pursue, and whether you simply give-up in the face of difficulties.

# 10
# Skills Tests

One of the properties of skills that we looked at earlier is that they can be tested to give you an objective assessment about how confident you should be in those skills. And if you can test a skill, you can not only observe that skill, you can measure and improve that skill.

A *skills test* is a test to see whether a person or organization possesses an ability required to perform some task, or achieve a goal. To avoid wishful thinking, and have real confidence that something will perform as expected, it needs to be tested to receive objective feedback on its performance. When an inventor draws up a blue print for an invention on paper, that inventor often does not know for certain that the invention will work until a prototype is developed and the invention is tested. This idea also applies to people, organizations, technology, or anything else you depend on.

The whole process of developing a skill begins with a test and observing the result. The first time you try anything, you will probably fail. But as you test your skills, you gradually figure out how to overcome your weaknesses and you build confidence in your ability to do it again. Your success or failure provides objective feedback that will tell you how much confidence to have in that skill and whether you need to continue developing it or stop wasting your time.

Different types of skills require different types of tests. Testing for an intellectual ability, like mathematical proficiency, is a relatively simple academic exercise. Traditional

Intelligence Quotient (IQ) tests attempt to measure and score general intelligence. The problem with general intelligence is that, in recent years, many Psychologists have agreed that, realistically, people have many types of intelligence, like visual intelligence or emotional intelligence. Any type of intelligence in this book is considered synonymous with intellectual ability. And intelligence in one subject does not necessarily transfer to having intelligence in another subject. In fact, a student may be highly proficient in Mathematics or History, but may be weak in other intellectual abilities, like judgement and critical thinking. That partly depends on the amount of time and effort put into developing those skills.

Most people do not test or measure their skills. So, their assessment of themselves, their self-confidence, and their evaluation of their own performance, is a matter of subjective opinion. To understand how that causes problems, imagine that James thinks he is a great singer. One evening, he steps onto the stage at a local karaoke bar and begins to sing. To his astonishment and surprise, he quickly realizes that people are laughing at him. So, afterwards, he decides to take singing lessons. People sometimes think about their own abilities in the same way that James did before he was laughed at, except they never receive feedback.

Rather than simply believing that you are an exceptional performer, if you put yourself to the test and measure your successes and failures, you will arrive at a more honest assessment about your true condition. To illustrate this, imagine Tim proudly tells his coworkers that he is going to run a marathon. A few days before the marathon, he decides to practice, runs a couple of miles, becomes exhausted, and gives-up. Naturally, Tim would lose confidence in his ability to run the entire marathon and realizes that if he tried, he may injure himself. Putting himself to the test kept him honest about his abilities. But, more importantly, Tim's judgment improved as a result of making a realistic assessment of what is possible in his own performance.

Or suppose Jill has never played golf, but thinks the game must be relatively simple. All you have to do is use the stick to hit the ball in the hole. How difficult could that be? So, the first time she plays, she performs terribly and admits she underestimated game's difficulty. That does not mean she will never be any good. And it does not mean she should give-up and never try again. You can build confidence in an ability by testing that ability, and making measurable progress with practice. Repeated successes should increase your confidence in your ability to do it again and, in some circumstances, make you more eager to repeat that success.

A colleague of mine once told me about his son who took up sky diving. At first, he was terrified to jump and did not think he could bring himself to do it. But after his first jump, sky diving became his new favorite past-time, and he could not get enough of it. When you gain greater confidence in your ability to perform an activity, especially when you enjoy it, you may become more eager and motivated to do it. And the activity, itself, may become an ongoing passion.

Skills tests are critical to making sure your performance is good enough to be successful. For example, if you remember a time when you studied for a test, and you quizzed yourself to see how many of the questions you could answer, you probably had some idea of how well you would do. If you answered all the questions correctly, then you had a high level of confidence in your ability to pass the exam. Psychologists call this the testing effect. Simply reading the material multiple times does not ensure you are able to recall that material at a later time. But if you test your ability to recall the material as you read it, you confirm that you are actually learning it.

To give another example, suppose John writes a speech and memorizes it. In his mind, he can imagine giving a spectacular performance before an audience that responds with rounds of applause. But as an amateur speaker who rarely gives public presentations, John has no idea how his performance will be delivered. As John gives the speech, he could remember it, but frequently stumbled along in his presentation. He told a joke that he thought would be received with rolling laughter and was, instead, received with rolling eyes. After delivering his speech and reflecting on his successes and failures, John was able to recognize areas needing improvement that could have improved his overall performance.

## 11
## Confidence Assessments

A confidence assessment is a way of numerically measuring how confident you are in something, which may include your abilities, or those of an organization or technology. One of the best ways to do a confidence assessment is to test an ability and calculate the rate of success or failure, which gives you a way to measure its development.

The success rate could be calculated by dividing the number of successful attempts by the total number of attempts. Zero percent indicates failure and would demonstrate a beginner, or introductory, level of ability. And one-hundred percent would be a success and would demonstrate an expert, or advanced, level of ability. Each attempt could further be divided into a percentage. If your success rate at completing a task is .9 and your failure rate is .1, then you could focus on that additional 10 percent to reduce your failure rate and get over the learning curve. If all one-hundred percent of your attempts are completed without error, you should have absolute confidence in your ability to succeed.

Calculating the success rates of organizational abilities can enable managers to make data-driven decisions about an organization's performance, and to avoid the wishful thinking that would result in false confidence and failure. This may involve testing product quality, response time, worker training, worker attitudes, or the whole end-to-end experience for customers and employees. The successes and failures that result from these tests will provide valuable feedback on areas of development that need more work. Without some type of confidence assessment, management really has no idea how the organization is performing and is more likely to suffer the consequences.

Confidence assessments can be especially useful in training. In many organizations, management will simply distribute information hoping that workers will read it and apply it to their jobs. But simply reading or memorizing information will not ensure that workers put those guidelines into practice. If management wants to ensure that occurs, they need to test employees and measure their success rate. It's better to test a worker's performance, and test the quality of that worker's production, to ensure that it meets sufficient quality standards without micro-managing. In other words, test-driven management gives management some idea of a worker's level of development. Workers who fail can be further trained in that specific area until the desired result is achieved. This way, management can gain a true sense of confidence, or lack thereof, in the organization's ability to perform as expected.

## 12
## A Theory of Mental Health

*Health* is the status of your overall physical and mental condition, and whether that condition is being strengthened or weakened. Strengthening certain types of abilities may actually improve your health. For example, physical wellness partly depends on the body's immune system to fight-off infections. Similarly, the mind can fight-off despair when a person has enough confidence in one's ability to overcome a significant challenge. And you can improve your ability to do that by strengthening abilities that make you more fit and confident in overcoming those difficulties.

My theory of mental health developed for this book is that as you develop your cognitive abilities, those parts of your mental condition strengthen, which can improve your ability to take-on difficulties, overcome adversity, and improve relationships, all of which can improve your outlook on life. Self-confidence, by itself, does not necessarily prevent, or cure, mental disorders. But it does provide opportunities for positive change, skills development, and personal relationships, which can reduce the negative conditions that give rise to, or exacerbate, mental disorders. So, goalsetting, combined with positive thinking, may help you strengthen your weaknesses, improve your resilience, and improve your mental health.

To understand mental health problems, we only need to look at studies on adversity, traumatic experiences, and significant losses, that cause a decline in a person's condition.

When looking at suicide risk factors, for example, as identified by the National Center for Injury Prevention and Control, they include things like substance abuse, a sense of helplessness, social and economic losses, and physical illness.[45] Researchers observed that life problems that caused significant stress and depression were the reasons young people wanted to commit suicide. And people over the age of 65 wanted to commit suicide as a result of the loss of a spouse or a physical illness.[45] Each of these circumstances presents difficulties that a person may, or may not, overcome. But if a person has enough confidence in one's ability to resolve these difficult problems then, theoretically, that person could avoid the despair that leads to giving-up, along with any suicidal or self-destructive behaviors.

Self-confidence is something that young people, and especially children, have a problem with because they do not yet have enough life experience to have developed many of their intellectual abilities, and therefore lack real confidence to bravely and courageously handle life's difficulties. Young people are still dependent on the adults who do much of the legwork for them. So, developing a healthy skillset can lead to maturing into a healthy adult who is capable of avoiding feelings of helplessness, despair, anger, and frustration, which may be the source of mental health problems later in life.

Similarly, adults can make mental health gains from healthier life choices. Health science tells us that we can improve our overall condition, wellbeing, and prolong our lives by following the ritual practices of exercise, and engaging in mental and physical activities, and feeding our bodies a nutritious diet. Some activities that can improve your mental condition include learning, practicing, and skills development, all of which can improve your mental fitness and self-confidence in performing specific roles. This is not just something that happens to you. It requires effort. Just as an athlete improves physical performance by repeating an activity, like running or lifting weights, you are able to improve your mental performance by repeating mental exercises that develop cognitive abilities. This improved mental fitness enables you to overcome situational challenges, be resilient during difficult times, and more confidently achieve life goals. Consequently, you will see improved mental health, improved self-esteem, psychological security, improved emotional attitudes, more work opportunities, and an improved outlook on life.

Lifestyle choices cause your health to improve or decline in other ways. For example, brain function is shown, in many studies, to improve as a result of eating a healthier diet and getting regular physical activity. Brain function may also improve as a result of forming new memories and engaging in other cognitive exercises that make you more mentally fit in performing those activities. Just as the body's performance fitness may improve with physical exercise, the brain's performance fitness may improve with mental exercises, daily practices, and skills development. As you test your performance, and work on weak areas, you can strengthen your performance in various roles.

If you are truly confident in your ability to conquer the difficulties of life, then why would you ever have a reason to despair and give-up? Only when a person lacks confidence in abilities, like social skills, does one feel helpless to do anything about one's social situation. And that could certainly lead to feelings of loneliness and helplessness. But if you perceive yourself as fully capable, and you are willing to put in the time and effort required to overcome those weaknesses, you could avoid those symptoms and improve your mental health.

## 13
## Developmental Problems

*Developmental problems* prevent the development of healthy life skills. They can be caused by conditions or life circumstances that result in developmental deficits, like undeveloped abilities, a lack of personal skills, critical thinking skills, or stress management skills. And people can actually develop maladaptive learned responses, or learned reactions, that are not helpful, and make them less effective in performing their roles. For example, a person may learn to have excessive distrust of people, or react negatively to personal interactions. These types of negative responses can develop, sometimes as a result of mistreatment or abuse. This maladaptive development is not helpful, does not help a person's social skills, and could lead to more serious mental disorders. This section looks at a few conditions, but certainly not an exhaustive list of conditions, known to cause developmental problems.

Children are most severely impacted by developmental problems because the child is still developing. Under-development, or abnormal development, can have a much more profound influence on the child's state of mind and behavior than an adult's. Young children are, especially, unable to be responsible for their own development because they do not have enough life experience to know how their development influences their life. They do not know how the world works, and cannot adequately make predictions or understand consequences. Because of factors beyond their control, children are at the mercy of, and absolutely dependent on, the adults who are expected to be responsible care-givers, who look after the child's safety and development.

People have many competing beliefs about the causes of abnormal development. Sadly, as we saw earlier in a section on mindsets, a person may even assume that someone who lacks an ability, is incapable of developing that ability. For example, it's not uncommon for children who have behavioral problems, depression, or substance use, to be prejudged as incapable of developing normally, when in fact, their full and healthy development was prevented by abuse or neglect.

Learning about the cause-and-effect relationship between conditions and developmental problems is certainly revealing. But people should avoid assuming too much about the causes of behavior until it is properly diagnosed by a doctor. Behavioral problems can certainly be developmental, but they can also be cause by brain injury, tumors, chemical influences, or other factors. For example, teenagers who have unintended pregnancies, according to the U.S. Department of Health and Human Services, have "reduced educational attainment and employment opportunity, greater welfare dependency, and increased potential for child abuse and neglect."[13] The report goes on to say that "teenage mothers are less likely to get or stay married, less likely to complete high school or college, and more likely to require public assistance and to live in poverty than their peers who are not mothers"…"The infants may be at greater risk of child abuse, neglect, and behavioral and educational problems at later stages."[13]

Developmental problems may include birth defects that are not genetic or chromosomal, but are caused by teratogens, which are substances, like alcohol, drugs, chemicals, or infections, that are completely preventable.[40] Low birth weight, in which a baby is born weighing less than 5.5 pounds, is sometimes caused by cigarette smoking, alcohol or illegal drug use, insufficient pregnancy weight, and multiple births. Low birth weight babies are at greater risk of "long-term disabilities, such as cerebral palsy, autism,"…"vision and hearing impairments, and other developmental disabilities."[14] Fetal alcohol syndrome, which is caused by the mother's alcohol consumption during pregnancy, can cause poor coordination, developmental disabilities, hyperactivity, psychiatric problems, and criminal behaviors.[10]

Developmental problems and, specifically, skills deficits, can be caused by severe adversity from a parent or pier who continues to create a hostile environment on a regular and, usually, daily basis. Just as an ability can be further developed, it can also be prevented from developing by isolating a person, preventing a person from interacting with people, keeping a person in conflict, or imposing control over the person's behavior and life choices.

These behaviors are more commonly found in abusive relationships. And rather than developing healthy cognitive abilities, the victim who has lived in an abusive relationship may develop social avoidance, cognitive deficits, behavioral problems, and mental disorders. Feelings of discouragement as a result of harsh treatment can cause persistent thoughts of giving-up and suicide, or believing that one is never good enough. In reaction to that treatment, a person may develop strong feelings of anger or depression that distort perceptions and lead to self-destructive or hostile behavior in place of, otherwise, healthy life skills.

Some forms of child maltreatment known to cause developmental problems include physical abuse, sexual abuse, child exploitation and corruption, emotional abuse, and neglect. Emotional abuse, according to American Humane, is known to cause problems with a child's conduct, as well as cognitive disorders, affective disorders, and other mental disorders.[3] Forms of emotional abuse may consist of calling the child something other than his or her name. The caregiver may verbally assault the child by ridiculing, verbally threatening, belittling, or bullying the child. The caregiver may terrorize the child by creating unrealistic expectations and threatening physical harm if the child doesn't live up to those expectations. And the caregiver may isolate the child, to prevent the child from interacting with people, which could reveal the abuse.

Children who were emotionally abused characteristically have persistent feelings of insecurity, problems forming relationships, a low self-worth, and self-destructive behaviors. The unstable environment created by an abusive caregiver can disrupt learning and cause emotional disorders that prevent the development of normal cognitive abilities, and prevent the child from pursuing normal life goals. Older children with severe emotional disorders may use substances to medicate those disorders, or may avoid people in general, including activities that promote healthy growth and development. These effects profoundly influence a person's life choices, like social activity, drug use, and educational attainment.

Abuse can occur when a parent becomes frustrated with a child's behavior and tries to increase punishment if the child does not respond according. This happens more commonly when caregivers have mental disorders and inflict uncontrollable violence. When those acts are repeated, unapologetically, it creates a mutually hostile relationship between the caregiver and child, where the child is constantly predicting, preparing for, and reacting to the parent's hostile behavior. These conflicts may be difficult, if not impossible to observe, if the parents are striving for social approval and behave differently around different people. The child may even hide the abuse to avoid losing the caregiver's support, and to avoid threats of violence made by the parent if the behavior is revealed.

A caregiver's behavior has an influence on the child's development in other ways. When a parent only punishes or disapproves of the child, it provides a hostile role model where the child only learns negative approaches to handling personal problems, and never learns or applies more constructive social skills. When a child is constantly responding to threats, is kept in a constant state of fear, sadness, or anger, it does not allow for the development of healthy personal skills. Instead of being cooperative, the child learns to be suspicious, defensive, and protective. And that lack of constructive social skills can interfere with future relationships with piers, instructors, and other adults.

Another common problem is that abused children, especially when they are emotionally abused and have emotional disorders, are often confused with spoiled children. People may attribute the child's crying to an unfulfilled demand when, in fact, it is an emotional disorder. Sadly, that assumption often leads to mistreating the child even more by adults or piers who bully the child. People who have emotional disorders, by the definition of the disorder, cannot control their emotions and often seek substances to sedate those emotions. Self-medication with illegal drugs leads to criminal behaviors that often result in law enforcement intervention.

This creates an impossible situation for the child who is

not mentally, emotionally, or socially developed, and is unable to make sense out of what is happening. The child's prefrontal cortex is not fully developed. So, the natural response is to fight-or-flee, to avoid the attack or counter-attack. These fight-or-flight responses to short-term conflicts, which may continue to be perpetuated by abusive caregivers or peers, can cause the child to make poor decisions that do not consider the long-term consequences.

If the child is under constant verbal attacks and criticism from adults or peers, and tries to fight-back, that rebellion may become so exaggerated that it develops into criminal behaviors. All the abusers have to do in their own defense, is point out the child's substance abuse, poor academic performance, behavioral problems, and poor decisions, as examples of mental defects or faulty genes.

Intervention does help, especially in circumstances where parents are committing other crimes or the child is in significant physical danger. But intervention can also be problematic. In the United States, people's right-to-privacy is protected. And if the child has no signs of physical abuse, or the abuser is not guilty of other crimes, then all the abuser has to do is deny the abuse, or put all the guilt and blame on the child. And that is easy when an abuser is respectable, keeps a clean home, and is polite. Once the child grows into an adult, the child is legally responsible for his or her behavior, even if the child is burdened with emotional problems, developmental deficits, and abnormal mental conditions resulting from childhood abuse.

The popular approach to treating behavioral problems or mental disorders appears to be punishment or medication. But if researchers could develop more effective programs that train on skills, like personal skills, critical thinking skills, responsibility, and stress management, it could not only help average children to be more effective in their life roles, it could help children with developmental deficits have an equal chance at a future. It could benefit people who lack the right type of encouragement during their formative years, or lack positive role models, or have severe behavioral or mental disorders resulting from abuse or neglect. Without some guidance on how to further develop their skills in everyday life, many of those people will be unemployed, incarcerated, or dead at a young age.

## 14
## Developmental Solutions

*Developmental solutions* to human problems are those that focus on developing the abilities required to solve a problem, achieve a goal, or more effectively perform a life role. Human problems have many causes that involve biology, neurology, biochemistry, brain anatomy, or developmental causes. And the job of the Doctor is to test for, and isolate, that cause. When human problems are developmental, rather than purely biological, they require developmental solutions, like a training program or goalsetting. And that requires the designer to understand how skills develop, why they fail to develop, how they influence a person's thinking, and how they solve problems.

Fixing developmental problems may require testing for developmental deficits or abnormal development. If a person has a communication skills deficit, developing those skills may improve that person's ability to perform roles in relationships. This is possible because researchers are able to test, observe, and measure different types of skills. Despite variations in the rate of development, researchers should be able to develop baselines, averages, and formulas for creating programs and regimens for training, instruction, child development, performance and fitness, public speaking, negotiation, crime reduction, and many other types of programs. By recognizing those skills deficits, the specialist should be able to prescribe a regimen aimed at developing targeted abilities to improve a person's overall mental condition and performance.

Developmental solutions provide a more permanent and lasting benefit, than quick and temporary solutions, like medication or punishment, because they help to strengthen skills that improve the subject's ability to effectively perform life roles, with practice, training, exercises, and learning. Many developmental solutions are already in use, today. For example, substance abuse and rehabilitation clinics teach life skills, like stress management, personal skills, leadership, and financial management, which enables the person to more effectively handle life challenges, and prevents the client from relapsing. Rather than copying what those programs are doing, this book presents the science behind those applications, to create more effective solutions.

The process of creating better developmental solutions involves testing and experimenting with different types of training approaches, to determine which one's are effective and which ones are not. Consideration needs to go into how skills are tested, measured, coached, or trained. If a researcher creates a program designed for criminal rehabilitation, does it actually change the thinking that lead to the criminal act? Does it work to resolve any underlying mental disorders, and develop the basic life skills required to maintain healthy relationships and hold down a job? If it does not, then the researcher should have no expectation in its effectiveness.

Consider a colleague of mine, Ian, who overcame a serious depression earlier in his life. During his early years, from early childhood to his early twenties, he was depressed and had frequent thoughts of suicide. During his early twenties, he experienced a series of life-changing events. He went from having low self-confidence and making average, or below average, grades in grade school and in college, to being a mostly straight-A student within a few years. He went from being depressed and hopeless, to feeling like he could do anything with no sign of depression for nearly twenty years, now. And today, Ian has a successful career.

Ian's case is interesting because his life did not change because of treatments commonly prescribed by mental health professionals, like medications, support groups, or therapy. He did not develop new relationships, overcome an addiction, or discover newfound financial opportunities. His life changed because of developmental factors that enabled him to improve his mental health, as a result of positive influences and guidance, and as a result of working toward his life goals. Therapy and support groups are tremendously beneficial and recommended for anyone who is experiencing life problems. And medication should never be ended without seeking the advice of a mental health professional. But Ian's case demonstrates why developmental solutions, rather than quick temporary fixes, should be considered as long-term solutions for treating the root causes of problems.

Developmental programs are equally valuable within organizations. A business's ability to remain profitable and achieve its goals entirely depends on the abilities of its workforce. So, if managers are able to test, and measure, those abilities, to assess the strengths and weaknesses of the organization, they can improve organizational effectiveness by developing targeted abilities within the organization, like communication skills or conflict resolution skills.

When hiring managers interview equally qualified candidates, the focus is often on what the candidate lacks, in terms of skills or personality, rather the candidate's potential for further development. If the business experiences a shortage of labor and the organization fails to perform, the blame is put squarely on the labor market. But managers could also take some responsibility for the future and performance of the organization by making sure it has the abilities necessary to be successful by actively working to develop talent from within.

## 15
## Research Challenges

Despite the vast amount of research contributed by talented professionals over the decades, the actual task of researching human behavior and creating replicable studies has proven to be challenging. Consider the fact that Social Psychologist Brian Nosek, and a team of over 260 researchers attempted to replicate the results of nearly 100 Psychological studies and found that only 39 percent could be reproduced.[8] Many researchers call this a replication crisis because it means that the results of those studies are not reliable. So, why, in an age of scientific and technological progress, where the public does not question the authority of the experts, is behavioral research so problematic?

Part of the problem is in the way behavioral researchers use Statistics, which can be a powerful research and decision-making tool if it is not misused. Statistical research is increasingly being used in the data sciences for applications, like data analytics, forecasting and predictions, machine learning, and artificial intelligence. These tools are used for predicting tends in things, like weather patterns, or financial markets, enabling business managers to make strategic business decisions about where to invest their money.

But while statistics is great for predicting trends in human populations, it is terrible at predicting an individual's behavior. Suppose a study found that, on average, people who exercise more than 3 times a week are more mentally healthy than people who do not. Obviously, an athlete could still develop a mental health problem, and a person who does not exercise may have no symptom of a mental health problem. That does not mean that study is worthless. You may feel better emotionally and physically if you exercised more the 3 times a week. But when the researcher begins to make inferences about risk factors based on statistical correlations, you ignore a vast number of extraneous influences on behavior that cannot be accounted for, which leads to inconsistencies and unreliable conclusions.

The biggest potential for the misuse of Statistics is in public and private industries that attempt to make predictions about individuals based on risk factors. For example, software is currently being used to predict the probability a person will repeat a criminal offense, or is likely to quit a job, based on risk factors. But having a high-risk factor for committing criminal offense, or quitting a job, does not mean you will do either one of those things. So, to make a decision against a person, either in terms of increasing a prison sentence, or influencing a hiring decision, may unfairly discriminate against that person based on grounds that really do not apply to the person.

Suppose, for example, a racial or ethnic group happens to makeup the majority of the prison population. That does not mean people who fit that racial profile are more likely to commit crimes. But if race or ethnicity were included as a risk factor, it would certainly subject a person to unfair treatment. Conclusions like these, when predicting a person's future behavior, are either true or false, right or wrong, correct or incorrect, not a 51% correct. And when those conclusions are incorrect, they are wrong and cause unfair biases, unfair discrimination, and unfair treatment. Decision-makers who use these products need to be aware that the businesses selling them are not financially incentivized to promote the negative impact that their products have on people's lives or communities.

Unfortunately, these types of problems are not new. During the early 20th century, nations like the United States and Nazi Germany conducted Eugenics programs that sought to rid populations of genetic defects. The Nazis used Eugenics as the justification for murdering millions of innocent people to purify the population of genetic defects. And in the United States, people who tested low on IQ scores, were considered to be high risk of having genetic defects and, in many cases, were sterilized without consent. Today, scientists recognize that people who have low IQ scores do not necessarily have a genetic defect. And even when looking at risk factors for conditions, like cancer, being at high risk does not guarantee the person will get cancer.

In his book entitled *Thinking Fast and Slow*, Nobel Prize winning Psychologist, Daniel Kahneman points out that people see patterns, and attribute causes, to random events.[32] To explain what he meant, Kahneman gave a hypothetical example of a study revealing that people who live in rural communities have a higher cancer-rate. Those findings, he said, may lead researchers to conclude that the higher cancer-rate must be due to an unhealthy and dirty rural lifestyle. Or, if the variables were changed and the study found a lower cancer-rate among rural residence, researchers may conclude that the lower cancer-rate was due to a healthy and clean rural lifestyle. People recognize patterns in random events, and attribute causes to those events.

Another problem with statistical research is that it does not reveal whether strong correlations are symptoms, or root causes. For example, statistical research has shown a strong relationship between loneliness and depression. Those findings show that social support and social relationships reduce stress, improve mental health, improve physical health, and even lower a person's mortality risk.[59] Based on this evidence, the researcher should conclude that loneliness is a likely cause of depression, which may influence a doctor's recommendation to a depressed patient.

Personal relationships provide many psychological and practical benefits, including providing a life-line of help in difficult situations, emotional support, and security in knowing that everything will be alright. When you spend time with people, you are creating positive experiences to reflect on. Being with people often evokes positive emotions and prevents people from dwelling on negative events. Social isolation, in contrast, allows a person to harbor negative feelings, dwell on negative memories, eat or drink excessively, or abuse substances as you have no direct obligation to remain sober, and potentially exacerbate existing mental disorders. Fulfilling your obligations to friends, family, or employers who need you, can give your life greater meaning and purpose. And the greatest benefit, of course, is having someone to turn to during times of need, if you need help, if you are lonely, stuck in a miserable situation, or are in an abusive relationship. Otherwise, you would have no recourse.

But people can be mentally healthy, even when they are socially isolated. So, inferring that loneliness causes depression may be, what a Psychologist would call, a confirmation bias, which is the tendency to seek evidence confirming a belief or theory, and filtering-out, or explaining away, contradictory evidence. Confirmation biases sometimes occur in Police investigations where detectives are required to build a case against suspects. And the easier it is to build a case, the more likely the suspect committed the crime. That tendency can create a problem when the detective becomes hyper focused on implicating the logical suspect without considering other possibilities, which may lead to convicting the wrong person. Or, another example would be when a Psychologist wants to secure a research grant for developing a pharmaceutical drug to treat a mental disorder. The researcher may only include evidence confirming the effectiveness of the drug, and exclude evidence suggesting otherwise.

Resolving human problems, in many ways, is similar to resolving computer problems. When a computer technician is presented with an error message, the technician does not always immediately know the cause of the problem. Some investigation, troubleshooting, and evidence collecting are required to test and replace faulty components. Similarly, a doctor cannot simply conclude that a person's depression has genetic origins without running a genetic test. If the doctor automatically presumes that depression has genetic origins and only prescribes medication, then the patient's problems may actually grow worse overtime.

So, concluding that a direct link between loneliness and depression exists while ignoring contradictory evidence would be another example of a confirmation bias. People can still develop depression when they are in close personal relationships, have low self-confidence, are in an abusive relationship, have a drug addiction, or have problems relating or communicating. In the local news, you can find examples of people who have many friends, close family, and may even be financially successful, who end up killing themselves and other people.[7]

You can also find case studies of people, like the seventeenth century Physicist and Mathematician Isaac Newton, or the twentieth century inventor Nikola Tesla, who lived and worked in almost complete isolation and lived into their mid-eighties. Additionally, having some alone time for thinking, reflecting, and personal development, has even shown to be beneficial to a person's mental health. If the specialist simply concludes that feelings of loneliness, or social isolation, is the root cause of depression based on the statistical evidence alone, prescribing more relationships may treat the symptom of the problem, which would have short-term benefit, but may never permanently treat the root cause of the disorder.

Confirmation biases are very common when trying to explain human behavior. For example, concluding that that people are naturally motivated by the need for self-preservation, despite instances of suicidal or self-destructive behaviors. Or most people would not cheat, or certain types of people are biologically predisposed to engage in harmful behaviors. Behavior is influenced by a wide variety of biological conditions, emotions, interests, and abilities, which are as unique to a person as a finger print, making it impossible to observe and account for every extraneous influence.

This is why laboratory research on human behavior is so problematic. The whole purpose of laboratory research is to control variables and understand contributing factors. But many variables involved with human development, like previous experiences, environmental influences, intellectual development, thinking processes, and memory, cannot be controlled. In surveys, participants tend to answer questions based on their available memory, which is susceptible to errors in recollection. Participants may feel judged, or may be dishonest or hide certain details, to conform to social expectations. Or a participant may have a low opinion of the survey and may lack interest in providing honest and thoughtful answers. Laboratory research also presents ethical concerns. Obviously, it would be unethical to replicate childhood abuse in a laboratory, to study its effect on the child's behavior and development. No matter how rigorously the researcher follows the Scientific Method, draws from the largest sample sizes to reduce the margin of error, or uses the most honest and unbiases participants, behavioral studies may continue to produce inconclusive results.

When studying human behavior, the world is your laboratory. Just like other creatures, you have to track people down to their natural habitat and observe them in action in their natural environment. This is what a research scientist may call Naturalistic Observation. And one way of studying applied Psychology is by studying how Psychology is already being applied. In a later chapter on motivational skills, for example, we look at how marketers influence buyer choices.

The most unbiased and objective research comes from real-world case studies that look at real-world causes and effects, or longitudinal studies that track people's development during a period of time. To understand abuse, for example, the researcher needs to study an actual subject who was abused, and how that subject recovered from the abuse. By slowly accumulating this collection of evidence from case studies, researchers should be able to gain a better understanding of the skills that enable people to be more effective in performing their life roles.

# CHAPTER II:
# WORLD MODELS

Much of what guides you in your thinking and behavior are the conclusions you form about reality. This chapter looks at why you form those conclusions, and why human judgement and decision-making is so limited. Specifically, this chapter looks at the colossal chasm between the mental logic people base their decisions on, and reality, and how that gap causes errors in thinking and problems in people's lives. The next chapter on critical thinking skills presents the solution to the problems presented in this chapter, and how those thinking skills can improve your ability to perform life roles.

## 1
## Cognitive Models

A cognitive model, or mental model, is a mental construct that represents how something in reality works. In other words, a mental model is an abstraction, or idea, that represents a real thing in the human mind. And that is not limited to individual things, but may include anything in your perception, including yourself, your thoughts, and your surroundings. Mental models are also called world models, or your mental picture of reality, or how you view the world through your mind's eye. They all refer to the same thing and are shaped by life experiences, education, culture, and other factors.

The idea that human perceptions are different from reality is an ancient one. Even in ancient Greece, Plato wrote about the Socratic paradox: "I know that I know nothing." And Plato went on to write about this theory of forms, which suggested that every object, like table, has a form, or idea, that represents that object in the mind. During the 16th century, Philosopher George Berkley, along with other famous Philosophers of his time, wrote about how objects existing in physical reality, exist only in the human mind as they are perceived by the brain and senses, which was an idea known as *immaterialism*. In other words, the world as you know it, is a mere mental representation of the real thing, created by sensory perceptions and represented by symbols. The mind, or consciousness, is an abstract representation of reality (i.e., a mental simulation) that is processed and stored by the human brain.

Mental models consist of many properties perceived by human biology, including sensory stimuli, memories, language, imagination, mental simulations, symbols, and dreams. From this raw input, people are able to see patterns, classify things into different types, and make predictions. These abilities are necessary for people to interact with, and live in, their environment. And that information can be used to build data models, mathematical models, and computer models, that can be used for scenario analysis, strategy, and planning.

Mental models usually improve as a person ages and learns from life experiences. For example, after you commute to a new job, you may be able to more accurately esti-mate and predict the next day's commute. As you gain ex-perience traveling to and from work, and recognize patterns in your commute, including accidents and rush-hour traffic, you can more effectively schedule your day and make bet-ter, and less regretful, scheduling decisions.

2
Limitations of Cognitive Modelling

Cognitive models are significantly limited because they are incomplete and inaccurate versions of the real thing and are often distorted by emotions. The logical conclusions people form in their brains, often have very little to do with reality. And that becomes a problem when people have difficulty distinguishing between perception and reality. In the minds of people, perception is truth, even when those perceptions are completely estranged from reality. And the true reality that exists beyond human perception, or the One Truth, is more of a strange and alien version of reality, than a shared and common experience.

When you observe any physical object, you are not see-ing a complete representation of the object but, instead, an incomplete and inaccurate representation constructed by your senses. Consequently, mental models cause mistakes in judgment and decision-making, and prevent people from fully understanding the consequences of their decisions. When you look at a pencil, you may be able to speculate about the materials that make-up that pencil. But you may have no idea about its chemical composition, how it was made, or where it came from. All that matters to you is that it is a pencil and you can write with it. To a child, that same pencil may become a microphone in an imaginary television show that is created purely out of the child's own mental simulations. The child, then, uses the pencil to simulate the experience of being a talk-show host.

Mental models are heavily influenced by hearsay and life experiences. People sometimes accept hearsay as truth without verifying it, especially when it comes from someone they trust, or have confidence in. Social media, news media, and commercial advertisements often try to create beliefs about a person or product, to influence people's political preferences and purchasing choices. And these influences may contain misinformation, inaccurate information, or incomplete information, which leads to misconceptions.

Criminals and con-artists exploit this weakness in judgment (i.e., people's tendency to believe what they are told) for illegitimate purposes. Collectors of antiques, sports memorabilia, or other collectables are sometimes duped into purchasing fraudulent merchandise. Or, a cybercriminal may use a tactic called social engineering, where the perpetrator pretends to be someone, like your bank or a family member, to get you to disclose personal information and steal your identity, or gain access to your financial accounts.

Mental models are also distorted by emotions, like anger or pleasure. Psychologists sometimes talk about people having an internal dialog, or narrative, which consist of stories that people tell themselves. For example, Tina is always angry because her boss is being a jerk. If Tina continuously tells herself the story of how her boss is a jerk, she will always harbor anger and resentment, even when she has nothing to be angry about. In her mind, her boss may be exaggerated into an evil villain or arch enemy. These distortions are also observable in phobias, when heights or insects are perceived to be deadly, even when those things are completely innocuous.

Since mental models are an incomplete, and largely inaccurate, mental representation of reality, intuition alone cannot enable people to know how reality works. That is why people created Science and the Scientific method. The physical world outside, and the lives that people live, have far more depth than meets the eye. When you look up into the sky, you may see an oxygen rich atmosphere, as you learned from your grade school education. But Science tells us that nitrogen, in fact, is the most abundant element in Earth's atmosphere. And while most people see one air mass, a Physicist may see microscopic particles that make-up many layers of gasses. That knowledge is not intuitively acquired from the senses, but learned from scientific instruments that detected and measured those gases.

Human history is filled with incorrect theories about the natural universe. Centuries ago, a dominant theory was that the world was flat and the universe revolved around the Earth. Since that time, exploration and photographic evidence has proven otherwise. The Scientific Method, itself, starts with a theory, which is nothing more than an unproven mental model of how a natural phenomenon works. The goal of the Scientist, then, is to prove, or disprove, that model to create a more accurate model of the structure, composition, and mechanical properties of Nature. And by creating a more accurate model, the human brain is able to more effectively work with and manipulate the properties of Nature. As our mental models of reality improve, so does our ability to improve the outcomes of decisions.

3

Memory

Cognitive models are stored in memory. The idea that people make decisions based on what is currently available in memory is a tendency Psychologists call the availability heuristic. The simple fact is, making decisions based on what is currently in memory is quick and convenient. So, when you decide what to eat for lunch, you may remember what you did in the past, or a local restaurant you dined at, or a commercial advertisement. Making decisions based on those memories makes decisions quick, efficient, and nearly effortless.

The problem with memory is that it is usually incomplete and inaccurate. And people usually do not accurately recall most daily, one-time, events in great detail. Recalling, or reconstructing, onetime experiences can be problematic, depending on your focus of attention and the amount of detail you observe and remember. To make since out of one-time experiences, people sometimes fill-in missing details to account for unknowns in a way that seems logical and plausible, which can create false memories.

Elizabeth Loftus and colleagues did a series of studies during the mid-1970s to explore this tendency in more detail.[37] In one of her studies, 100 students were asked about a film featuring a multi-car accident. The students were asked questions about things featured in the film, and things not featured in the film. Some questions were worded: "Did you see the _____?" which suggests that the subject appeared in the film. And others were worded: "Did you see a _____?" which suggests that the subject may have appeared in the film. Respondents were more likely to say they saw a subject when the question implied it was in the film.

This tendency to remember things differently based on suggestions, or circumstantial evidence, is a problem in police investigations if an eye witness gives an account that seems probable and likely because the witness, in fact, is unable to remember the event accurately. Police or prosecutors may try to build a plausible scenario. And in the process of doing so, they may inadvertently coerce a witness into giving false testimony.

Some one-time events may create stronger memories than others, like those that are highly impactful or world changing. Emotionally provocative events, like the birth of a child, a terrorist attack, or an event that evokes pain, sadness, pleasure, or awe, is shown, in some studies, to be recalled more vividly. While the reason for that is unknown, profound, life-changing, or world-changing, events usually cause people to reflect longer, think about, talk about, and explain those events, which serves to create a better mental record and a more accurate recollection of those events.

Memory can be improved. An actor, for example, can learn the lines of a play and recite them accurately with enough practice. You could fact-check your knowledge and correct yourself if you are incorrect. Or you could spend time learning and memorizing a subject so that when you are put to the test, you know the answers. Subject matter experts, whose profession involves applying knowledge to solving problems, can increase their professional value this way.

The ability to distinguish between strong and weak memories is a critical skill that keeps people honest about themselves and their world. Even if you do not mean to lie, an inaccurate memory can be construed as a lie since it is not an accurate representation of the truth. The ability to distinguish between what you know and do not know is a critical thinking skill that we look at in the next chapter that can enable you to reduce mistakes and more effectively create wanted outcomes.

# 4
# Decision-Making

Before getting further into how cognitive models influence decisions, we need to understand how decision-making works. A decision, as it is defined in this book, is an action or inaction. It could involve applying a solution to a problem, or responding to an opportunity or threat. And decisions are highly contextual and apply to specific skillsets. For example, an automotive mechanic may be able to make a more knowledgeable, and informed, decision about vehicle maintenance, troubleshooting, and purchases. But that improved decision-making does not transfer to interior design, which requires a different skillset.

Decision-making is also highly influenced by the options and opportunities that people have. Anytime you have more than one option, or opportunity, you have a choice. For example, you have a choice about whether to act or not, whether to be happy or sad, or whether to be mean or nice. You can choose what you want to eat for dinner the next evening. But you may decide to do something else. Having more than one option to choose from can improve your decision making, but only to a diminish extent. Having too many options can be overwhelming, and may cause you to make a random choice that results in a poor decision.

Judgment involves how you assess, or evaluate, different options or opportunities. And your judgment influences your decision-making. If you think a person is likeable, that judgment will influence your decision about whether you interact with that person. If Susan decides she does not like a coworker, she may refuse to cooperate with him. And that lack of cooperation can lead to project failures, miscommunication, and organizational disfunction. Rather than focusing on the inevitable consequences of cooperating with her coworker, Susan is focusing on her dislike of the coworker. Human judgment does not have to be based on whether something is likeable. It could also be based on numbers, factual assessments, or whether a decision would result in wanted gains, or unwanted losses.

Decision-making also involves understanding cause-and-effect relationships between decisions and their consequences. Anytime a person makes a decision that hurts people, or causes some negative consequence, we could say that the person made a poor decision. The ability to recognize and predict these consequences is fundamental to improving decision-making. For example, if you could accurately predict that a decision would result in negative outcome, you could prevent that negative outcome. If you accurately predict that a decision would result in positive outcome, you could work harder to bring about that outcome. So, making good decisions required enough knowledge to predict whether a decision will result in a positive or negative outcome. And the next chapter on critical thinking skills introduces some ideas on how to improve that ability.

People's lives are actually very predictable. If you are a college student, you could predict that if you do not study for an exam, you will fail. That decision to study also has higher-order consequences, like failing the class, dropping out of school, and losing the investment in your education. The ability to predict consequences, like worst-case scenarios, can be especially motivating. If you ever worried about being late to an appointment, or worried about not passing an exam, those worries could motivate you to try harder, to be more knowledgeable, and create a more desirable outcome. You simply cannot understand where you will end-up if you do not see where you are going.

Effective decision-making absolutely depends on the ability to predict the consequences of a decision. The inability to do that usually results in unintended consequences. For example, when a politician proposes a law that appeals to the anger and sentiments of voters, without considering the negative impact it will have on the community or its economy. Or a business owner who wants to increase profit margins begins selling substandard products that puts people lives at risk.

Often people focus primarily on their own immediate interests without considering, or caring about, all of the consequences of their decisions, including how their decisions impact other people's lives. For instance, suppose Susan is experiencing financial problems and sees bank robbery as the solution. Since bank robbery puts lives at risk, and causes significant losses to the community by redirecting resources, like law enforcement and money from other community needs, and would result in a prison sentence, that is not the best solution to Susan's financial problems.

In another example, if Tim, who is a Sale's associate, does not meet his quota, he will lose a bonus, or maybe his job. So, he uses deceptive tactics to get people to buy things they do not need, like automatically enrolling someone in an unwanted service. Or, a business manager may withhold negative information, like revenue losses, from investors to increase investment in the business. Each of these creates a situation in which someone experienced an unfair loss or was negatively impacted by the decision, whether it was an unsuspecting customer or an unsuspecting investor. And those people may be motivated to protect their interests by filing a complaint or seeking legal representation.

The whole purpose of skills training, whether it is job training, emergency response training, or any other form of training, is to improve outcomes. Not having certain skills would prevent a person from solving problems that require those skills.

5

Executive Function

Decision-making also has a biological component in that it's controlled by the Executive Function of the brain (i.e., the Prefrontal Cortex), that controls whether to commit an act or not. This area of the brain controls how you manage time, plan your day, and where to focus attention, and controls complex planning, strategy, problem solving, social behavior, and goal-oriented behavior. All of these behaviors involve understanding the consequences of actions.

Research has shown that an underdeveloped, or low functioning, Prefrontal Cortex may be attributed to poor judgment and risky behavior. According to Laurence Steinberg, who does Functional Magnetic Resonance Imaging (or fMRI) research, in a story by National Public Radio on the teenage brain, adolescents often try to act in their best interest, but sometimes make poor decisions because their judgment is influenced by hormones and peer pressure when in the company of peers.[58] So, while the Limbic System (i.e., the emotional and impulsive part the brain) is always motivating a person to take action and look out for opportunities and threats, the Prefrontal Cortex (i.e., the logical and rational part of the brain) tries to restrain the Limbic System with logic and reason. And according to research by Neuroscientist B. J. Casey, who was also featured in the story, since adolescents have not developed that logic and reason, they uninhibitedly fight threats and pursue opportunities, resulting in poor decisions.[58]

Some of this may be attributed to the fact that adolescents have not developed the learned intellectual abilities and life skills necessary to approach problems constructively. And in fact, adults behave similarly when they are presented with uncertainty and face the prospect of severe loss or harm. They may, consequently, react very emotionally and irrationally out of desperation to prevent a negative outcome.

Brain damage, or a significant decline in brain function, in the Executive area of the brain can also cause a lack of motivation, poor decisions, or exhibiting inappropriate social behaviors. According to research by Neuroscientist Antonio Damasio and his colleagues, people with damaged frontal lobes tend to lack normal emotional responses. These emotions, according to their research, play a significant role in motivating decisions.[44] People commonly associate emotions with irrational behavior, like anger leading to an impulsive and irrational act. But, according to Damasio's research, emotions are also constructive and motivating, for example, when a person is motivated to change things that cause unhappiness and anger. The argument could even be made that emotions play a role in creativity, in motivating a person to create new things that evoke positive emotions.

6
Thought Processes

*Thought processes* are how the human brain processes information and forms conclusions. People tend to use *intuition*, or gut-instinct, which is the human brain's default mode of thinking based on what is present in the mind or the environment. Intuition enables you to act, rather than being too bogged down by the details when assessing and evaluating situations. For example, determining whether a vegetable is good to eat only requires a little common sense to see, smell, and taste the vegetable. You could research how long a vegetable lasts or consult with an expert. But without smelling or tasting the item, that information will not tell you whether the vegetable is actually good to eat.

Psychologists Amos Tversky and Daniel Kahneman, who are famed for their studies on how the brain processes information, proposed that when people are faced with uncertainty, they use shortcuts they called heuristics. These are intuitive techniques, or rules of thumb, that guide people's choices and enables to brain to operate more efficiently, to avoid getting bogged down by the details. For example, if you were forced to make a choice among the many different cereals at a Supermarket, and want to reduce your chances of purchasing one you do not like, you may use a familiarity heuristic and choose a brand you are familiar with, instead of one you know nothing about. Or you may use an availability heuristic and choose the cereal that is most available in your memory, maybe the one you saw on the billboard as you walked into the store.

Amos Tversky and Daniel Kahneman also proposed that people's choices are influenced by cognitive biases (i.e., the tendency to favor one option over another). All people have things they like or dislike. But biases, as Tversky and Kahneman pointed out, often leads to mistakes in how the brain processes information. For example, suppose you are a manager tasked with maximizing profit. Your boss presents you with two profit maximizing strategies. From your education, you know that Strategy A maximizes profit, but you do not know anything about Strategy B. So, you choose Strategy A, not knowing that Strategy B is the more effective strategy. Rather than weighing your options and making a truly informed and unbiased decision, your decision was biased towards Strategy A for reasons only known to you.

Cognitive biases are not necessarily harmful, when making most daily low-risk, low-impact, decisions, like choosing what to eat or how to dress, or if you like a certain food because it is delicious. If you had a negative experience with a product that caused you to lose money, it may influence your decision to avoid it in the future. Or, if you live in a democracy, like the United States, you may support a political candidate because that person represents your political beliefs. These are all examples of healthy biases.

But people also have unhealthy, or harmful, biases. For example, believing that you have greater abilities than you do, or deceiving yourself into believing that luck, or some advantage, is on your side. A gambler, for example, may not know the outcome of a bet. But he, at least, knows he must gamble to win. This remains true, even when he continues losing all of his money while remaining biasly optimistic that he will eventually win it back. Psychologists call this tendency to think that future probabilities are altered by past events, the Gambler's Fallacy. For example, if a coin-flip lands on heads five times in a row, a person may predict that the next flip will land on tails, despite the fact that the probability remains unchanged.[31]

People also have a belief bias in which they believe ideas that conform to their cognitive model of how the world works, and disbelieve those that do not. If a statement does not conform to one's mental logic about how things are supposed to work in reality, that person simply does not believe it. Or, a person may have a normative bias based on cultural values in which people are judged, and even discriminated against, based on lifestyle choices, like whether they get married, have a family, or whether they serve in the military.

# 7
# Harmful Biases

Harmful biases are those that are unfair, or harmful, to people. For example, making an assumption about a person that does significant damage to the person's reputation or career, which results in property loss, physical harm, or wrongful employment termination.

The ability to distinguish between right and wrong (i.e., the conscience), is rooted in human judgment and is the foundation for the moral standards. When your judgment about someone is wrong, it can result in harm and unfair losses that could be considered morally wrong as well. People are more likely to behave unethically when they pursue their own interests at the expense of others. An example would be a manager who is more concerned about making the business profitable by producing an inferior product, rather than making one safe for consumption. Producing a substandard product may save money and increase profit in the short-term. But the long-term consequences may include a decline in revenue and profits when buyers lose trust in business and its products.

Another example in which poor judgment causes harm is when a person is wrongfully convicted of a crime. Detectives are required to build a case against potential suspects. Logically, suspects that are easier to build a case against are more likely to have committed the crime. But detectives can go too far when they continue building a case against the wrong person, usually because the detective is convinced that the suspect is guilty and focuses on finding evidence to secure a conviction. Suspects, who may be children, people with mental disabilities, or people impaired by drugs or alcohol, may even confess to the crime after being subjected to an exhausting interrogation and promised a reduced sentence, or the ability to prove one's innocence later.[30]

Superficial appearances, according to research by Psychologist Alexander Todorov, can significantly influence how people are judged. In a study, he asked participants to compare the portraits of candidates seeking election in both the House and the Senate and to judge their competence. The participants predicted the election's outcome more than 70% of the time, suggesting that facial features, rather than qualifications or expertise, can bias voter's judgment of candidates. These types of biases, he suggested, may also influence hiring or promotion decisions.[33]

Hiring managers can judge candidates by criteria other than qualifications and proven expertise, even in skills-based professions. A hiring or promotion decision, for example, may be based on whether the person looks or acts the part, knows the business processes, has an existing relationship with management and coworkers, rather than whether the person has proven skills and competencies required to perform the work. This form of discrimination would be a prejudice, or a pre-judgment, in which people are making a judgment before they have all the facts necessary to make an informed decision.

In recent years, many publicly recognizable employers like Google, Facebook, and Starbucks, have made efforts to reduce harmful biases in their workplace by enrolling employees in unconscious bias training programs, and usually in response to negative publicity.[36] The purpose of these programs is to teach workers how to treat people fairly, and to not have a negative basis against people based on superficial appearances.

Harmful biases can creep into workplace decisions in other ways. For example, a hiring manager may predict that a person who was jobless for the last three months probably does not want to work. Or a person who is working an entry level job probably does not have any qualifications or experience. A manager may, then, decide to not even bother reading the applicant's résumé, even when the applicant is truly a highly skilled and experienced professional who had an unfortunate series of events. The hiring manager, in that instance, is prejudging based on pattern recognition and categorization, without doing the work to find out why those patterns exist.

Or suppose a job candidate had seven jobs during the last seven years. The hiring manager may conclude that the candidate is unable to hold down a job. Having seven jobs in seven years may indicate a problem, but not necessarily with the job candidate if that person is consistently overqualified, highly skilled, had great relationships with coworkers, and resigned on good terms.

People also have belief biases that can be harmful. People simply do not want to believe that certain individuals behave contrary to their public image and the mental model they have of the person. People also have an authority bias, and automatically trust that an authority figure would never victimize another person. But if an authority figure is an abuser, and is victimizing people in some way, maybe a man is slipping women a date-rape drug and committing rape, people may decide the accusation is too unbelievable based on what they know about the person in question.

People have, what some Psychologists would call, a just-world-hypothesis in which they believe that people get what they deserve and good reasons exist for everything. But you will find both good reasons and terrible reasons, and sometimes horrific reasons, for why things are the way they are. So, simply because a person is in an unfortunate situation does not necessarily mean that a good reason exists for it.

Harmful biases can also be systemic in organization, like the criminal justice system. Policies, like mandatory sentencing laws, can prevent judges and officials from using their own judgment when deciding cases. Consequently, people are convicted of minor offenses, like victimless misdemeanor crimes, and face severe punishments, like being branded felons for life. When you consider that the Felony label was created for perpetrators of serious crimes, like murder, rape, or high-crimes, the branding convicts the person of a much more serious crime, at least in the public mind.

Biases in statistical probabilities also lead to unfair discrimination. When used ethically, statistics can be an extremely valuable branch of Mathematics, which is increasingly being used by Data Scientists to develop AI, Machine Learning, and Big Data to recognize patterns and make predictions that people would not be able see, otherwise. But creating a technology solution is not the same thing as creating a responsible technology solution that is ethical and moral. And software that makes inferences from statistical data may be great for predicting trends in populations, but as we have already seen is terrible at predicting the behavior and tendencies of individuals.

In at least nine states in the United States, software is currently being used to help Judges assess the statistical risk factors of an offender repeating a crime when deciding a sentence. A recent ProPublica article found that numerous black defendants, who did not go on the reoffend, were rated as a much higher risk than white defendants who did. In one case, a young black woman convicted of petty theft was rated as a high risk, while a white man previously convicted of armed robbery was given a low risk assessment. While the maker of the software said that the algorithm does not consider factors like race, they said it does consider factors like education level, employment, parent's criminal record, and friend's drug use.[6]

Only a certain percentage of people who had parents who were criminal offenders go on to commit crimes. And many crimes are caused by impaired thinking resulting from substance use disorder. Among those people, a certain percentage may, or may not, be abusing substances to medicate mental disorders. And a certain percentage of those problems may be resolved by the time the person matures into adulthood. So, when you do the math, if only 3 percent of the population, out of one hundred thousand, were considered high-risk, but do not go on to reoffend, then that would be 30 thousand people who were unfairly sentenced.

These types of systems are not only being used in the Criminal Justice system, they are being used to determine whether you get a loan, and in hiring or promotion decisions. At a TEDx event in 2017, robotics researcher Peter Hass pointed out that similar systems may be used to decide whether you get a loan or a job interview.[26] And in fact, a large distributer of Human Resources software recently released a product that would allow employers to predict whether an employee is likely to quit, which could be used to discriminate against job applicants.

The results of a statistical study may have nothing to do with a person's choices or future decisions. But they may be used against people to determine whether they get a loan or job. These systems may even go so far as to include genetic risk factors to determine health insurance premiums. In some ways, this is like Eugenics 2.0. But, instead of sterilizing or killing a person because of a low IQ score, people are being discriminated against for having certain risk factors, which may have nothing to do with their own unique actions or condition.

For example, you may have a genetic profile that suggests that you are at high-risk of a mental disorder or cancer, despite the fact that you have never had a problem with mental disorders and have never been diagnosed with cancer. But if an employer has access to that information, directly or indirectly through a third-party, that employer could use that information to mitigate risks, to simply exclude people from employment who present a high-risk profile.

# 8
## Decision Logic

Human decisions follow a pattern similar to propositional statements, which follow the conditional logic that goes something like: if some condition (y) is true, then do (x). If your brain receives a signal that your body is hungry, your brain has learned to respond by executing the instructions "if hungry, then eat" which mobilizes you to eat or drink. Or, if the proposition "the weather is too cold" is true, then stay inside.

This conditional logic is similar to how an instruction set controls a computer program. In computer programming, these types of conditional statements are called flow control statements because they control the program's behavior. They consist of if-then-else statements, while loops, for-each loops, and other types of decision statements, which can be diagramed using a flow chart, similar to one a software engineer would use to design a program.

An example of this type of conditional logic may be: if you do not study, you will fail the exam. Or, if the time is 10pm, then go to bed, else watch the news. While the time is between 10pm and 6am, sleep. For each page in the book, read to end. People establish routines and procedural logic in their decisions as a way of programming their lives to make complicated decisions easier and more automatic, recognizing that certain conditions need to be met to achieve certain goals. You may schedule time, plan the day, and program a series of activities, to help you achieve specific ends. Or, if you want to stay fit, then create an exercise regimen for engaging in physical activity a few days a week.

Expressing behavior in the form of propositional statements can be useful for testing, observing, measuring, and improving a person's judgment and ability to apply critical thinking skills, which is a subject we look at in the next chapter. For example, you could test a person's critical thinking skills by presenting a series of propositional statements that the person is required to evaluate to true, false, or inconclusive. These critical thinking skills tests could help identify and address logical errors in thinking.

9

Logical Errors

A *logical error* is a mistake in how the brain processes information. People have a tendency to arrive at incorrect conclusions and make mistakes, when they make decisions based on incomplete, or inaccurate, information. The propositional statement "if some condition (x) is true, then some other condition (y) must also be true" can lead to wrong conclusions. For example, if Susan left her job, then she must have performed poorly. Or one could further conclude that if Susan performed her job well, then her employer would want her to stay and would promote her. Both of these conclusions could be false because how well Susan performed her job may have nothing to do with the reason she left. That logic infers that condition (y) exclusively depends on the condition (x), when the two have no relationship.

People also use probability as a heuristic in lieu of actual numbers and information because of limitations in time and resources. For instance, if everyone is subscribing to a service, then it must be worth subscribing to. Or if no one is subscribing to a service, then it must not be worth subscribing to. This probabilistic strategy enables people to protect themselves from the risk of loss, and quickly make decisions when they lack time to research every option. But it quickly leads to mistakes in reasoning.

When decisions are high-risk, high-impact, decisions, using mental logic without investigating reality is not the most reliable approach because the decisionmaker cannot know the consequences of the decision. A business manager may try to increase profit by using cheap materials to produce an inferior product. But that may, inadvertently, lose customers. Or, a politician with good intentions may create a program that leaves a community without the funding necessary to finance critical infrastructure. In each of these, the decisionmaker is arriving at logical, propositional, conclusions based on good intentions, but may not be putting enough effort into investigating the real-world consequences, to reduce uncertainty about the outcome. This form of thinking is what I call, thinking without thinking. Forming beliefs, being skeptical to protect yourself, or simply believing someone you trust, are all forms of thinking without thinking.

## 10
## Applied Models

Cognitive models are easier to work with when they are expressed in an observable form and documented. Writing down an idea on paper makes it easier to study, research, improve, and share with other people, than an idea that is completely abstract. This is especially true when collaborating with a team. Ideas are easier to explain and talk about if you have a diagram, blue prints, data models, or mind mapping.

Designers in many industries rely on multiple forms of communication, design plans, diagrams, and blueprints, which can be reviewed to make calculated decisions and prevent errors and mistakes. As an example, suppose a project manager of a software engineering team has a new project. The client requesting the software knows what he wants, but is very short on details. He only provides very brief and vague description of the proposed solution. To tackle these difficulties, the project manager makes drawings, wireframes, mockups, and user stories, to illustrate how the software will be used. He, then, tests his models by showing his client the plans, and makes necessary corrections to the plans long before a significant amount of budgeted time, money, and resources are spent developing the solution. This is an example of how a project manager effectively reduces uncertainty, in terms of project requirements, and guarantees the success of the project.

Documenting the cause and effect relationships of decisions and their consequences enables people to further analyze, brainstorm possibilities, and research those relationships. That could be accomplished by creating an interdependence map, cause-and-effect diagram, or an input-output diagram, to understand the initial consequences, along with all the higher-order consequences.

Another common application of modeling is using data models to solve complex problems. Mathematical models, for example, can be used to make predictions and do scenario analysis. A researcher could calculate the population growth rate and the sales of polluting products to understand what humanity's dystopian future will look like and devise strategies on how to avoid it. Business models are often written down in the form of a business plan, which helps the entrepreneur do cost/benefit analysis, and study the factors influencing the success of the business. Solving these problems on paper, beforehand, is far easier than dealing with costly negative consequences after-the-fact.

In his book *Principles: Life and Work*, Ray Dalio, wrote about the principles that made his billion-dollar investment firm, Bridgewater, successful and the hard, and sometimes painful, truth about running a successful organization.[12] As a side note, at the time of Ray's retirement as Chief Executive Officer and Chief Investment Officer in 2017, Bridgewater controlled about a $160 billion in assets. Part of what made his company successful, according to Ray, was that, starting early in his career, he would take notes about the factors influencing market conditions. For example, he would observe cause-and-effect relationships between things, like rain fall, crop yields, and the price of feed for livestock. Or he would observe the effect of federal policy on interest rates, or how the demand for specific products influenced demand for commodities and precious metals. He would, then, write computer programs based on these data models to input different factors and run different scenarios. And overtime, they would gradually yield more accurate predictions about financial markets when making investment decisions. Ray said this was an ongoing cycle of trying, failing, learning from failures, making improvements, and trying again. And, despite not always being accurate, the market and investment models Ray created during his decades at Bridgewater helped the business make better predictions and better investment decisions.

Computer models are becoming increasingly more reliable for scenario analysis, project planning, automating redundant tasks, and performing complex calculations when making predictions. Structural engineers use computer models to analyze how environmental factors, like earth quakes and hurricanes, will impact the structures they are designing. Weather forecasters use computer models to understand factors influencing weather conditions when making predictions. But these predictions are only as accurate as the models upon which they are based. If those models do not contain enough relevant information about influencing factors, or the cause and effect relationships between those factors, they will not be reliable.

# CHAPTER III:
# CRITICAL THINKING SKILLS

The previous chapter looked at some problems with human judgment, and why it is prone to errors in thinking and costly mistakes. In this chapter, we look at how developing critical thinking skills can help you overcome limitations in judgment and reduce uncertainty as a decisionmaker.

People develop skills to solve problems. And the inability to develop critical thinking skills can result in a variety of social problems. People normally think of social problems as things, like crime, abuse, poverty, and substance addiction. But average people cause less obvious social problems when their assumptions negatively impact people's lives, if they damage a person's reputation or career. For example, if a report is filed to the Police Department, or a Human Resources department, and it is not taken seriously, the result could be unnecessary death, serious injury, or a loss of employment.

This chapter looks at the critical thinking skills necessary to overcome the limitations in human judgment presented in the last chapter. While you may not use all of the techniques presented in this chapter, my hope is that you become familiar with them to become a better critical thinker.

Many of these techniques are used by professionals in industries when thinking about difficult problems, or taking on complex projects.

# 1
# Critical Thinking

*Critical thinking*, as I will define it in this book, is a process of forming a judgment based on objective facts and research. This requires people to be able to distinguish between mental logic and reality. And as we saw in the last chapter, that is an ability that people struggle with and is a skill that needs to be developed. In this chapter, we look at different techniques for reducing uncertainty in decision-making, to more accurately predict the consequences of decisions. Some of those methods include interacting with people, asking questions, doing research, conducting tests, consulting with experts, and getting the facts necessary to know what you are talking about.

Critical thinking consists of two fundamental abilities: 1) recognizing knowledge gaps, and 2) doing the work to fill-in those knowledge gaps. People are often reluctant to suspend their judgment, or admit they lack knowledge about something. And that can cause people to form assumptions, and make poor decisions, that have a negative impact on people's lives. You cannot know what you are doing if you do not know what you are talking about. And knowing what you are talking about requires time and effort, to ask questions, do research, and obtain the necessary facts. When predictions are based too much on mental logic, rather than observable evidence, it leads to mistakes and errors that can cause financial losses, job losses, and lost lives.

Suppose, for example, you want to purchase a vehicle

you found on a website. The vehicle is attractive, has low miles, and is reasonably priced. So, you want to buy it right away before someone else does. The problem is, you have no idea what you are getting. You have no idea how it runs, whether it was in an accident, whether it was well maintained, and what parts were replaced. You may end up purchasing a vehicle that will not start. And you may have to put in a considerable amount of money to fix it. If you are a mechanic, or know someone who is, you could inspect the vehicle to make a more informed decision. But simply because a vehicle looks attractive in a picture, does not mean that it is a good choice. Purchasing that vehicle, then, would have a lot of uncertainty and risk.

## 2
## Suspending Judgment

*Suspending judgment* is a critical thinking skill that involves collecting more evidence about the cause of a problem and its solution before forming your final judgment based on the facts you find. Consider a recent Dateline story on NBC about a college student who was killed after calling the police department multiple times to report her boyfriend was threatening her life. The case was never investigated and, sadly, her boyfriend ended up murdering her.[39] This tragedy could have been avoided if the police would have looked at the problem seriously, questioned relevant people, and did an investigation to find out the truth. Her murder was directly attributed to a lack of critical thinking skills on the part of those who received the report.

The modern world is one where you could be victimized by con-artists, cybercriminals, and others who want to steal from you. And because of that, people learn to be skeptical as a way of protecting themselves. But just because something seems unbelievable, does not mean it is untrue. If you, instead, suspend your judgment and admit when you do not know something, you will be correct and will harm no one. But the moment you believe that someone is lying or overreacting, then you have far more potential to cause negative consequences.

Suspending your judgment, and admitting you have a knowledge gap, requires being honest about your own abilities, and not being too overly confident, when making decisions that present risk or harm. This self-doubt, and questioning whether your judgment is correct, can be beneficial when it enables you to avoid, or prevent, mistakes that cause substantial losses, like investing millions of dollars in a business venture without any prior knowledge about the business. If you suspect that your judgment may be incorrect, it should motivate you to collect more information, do more research, or use some other critical thinking skills to reduce uncertainty in that decision.

3

The Uncertainty Reduction Principle

The previous chapter looked at how people default to intuition when making decisions. And that is fine for most daily low-risk, low-impact, decisions. But intuition, alone, does not always provide enough information to correctly arrive at conclusions, since intuition tends to be based on inaccurate and incomplete information. So, to mitigate that risk, you have to do two things. You have to recognize a knowledge gap (i.e., a what you do not know), and then think to collect enough information to fill-in that knowledge gap. You have to ask questions, do research, look at facts, and find out the truth. Relying on mental logic alone, or simply believing hearsay, without thinking to look into the truth, can lead to costly mistakes. And you can reduce those mistakes by applying the uncertainty reduction principle.

The uncertainty reduction principle states that since you risk not have enough information to produce the desired outcome, you can mitigate that risk by seeking more information. But at some point, you have enough information to make a decision, and no additional information will optimize the final decision or its outcome. Any student of economics will recognize this as the Law of Diminishing Returns, which refers to the idea that as you increase the amount of input in the production of a good, holding all other inputs constant, the output also increases. But at some point, no matter how much of that input you add, the amount of output begins to diminish.

To understand this idea, when you initially begin to collect information about a choice, even a small detail could dramatically change your choice from one extreme to another. For example, suppose Margaret is moving to a new city and is trying to make a decision about whether to move to the neighborhood of Towering Oaks or Winding Trails. She really wants to live in a safe neighborhood that is close to her child's school. And the housing in Towering Oaks is considerably less expensive and closer to a school. But after doing some online research, she discovers that Towering Oaks has one of the highest crime rates in the city and that Winding Trails is one of the safest. So, despite not getting exactly what she wanted, her research helped her to make the most satisfactory decision.

The question is: How much information do you need to avoid making mistakes? Psychologists have found that people tend to believe that their choices are more informed than they are, which they call a choice-supportive bias. You could, for example, smell a vegetable to make sure it's not spoiled. But you cannot always detect if water is contaminated with unsafe levels of lead or arsenic. And while you may have no reason to be concerned about your drinking water, people underestimate how oblivious they are about the world they live in and have full confidence in their water, even when they have no idea what is actually in it.

4

Quality of Information

*Quality of information* (QOI) refers to the accuracy and value of information. People have greater certainty in their conclusions when those conclusions are based on information known to be true and accurate. If you ask someone for directions, and you are given the wrong directions, you will probably not get to your destination any faster by following those directions.

Some of the qualities that can degrade the quality of information include truthfulness, hearsay, and cognitive biases. People largely learn how the world works from hearsay (i.e., what they are told), from friends, family, instructors, news, and other information sources. The problem with hearsay is that it is not always true because of memory loss, emotions, beliefs, exaggerations, misunderstandings, or a deliberate effort to manipulate the facts. Cognitive biases degrade the quality of information when people ignore, or filter out, a considerable amount of information that does not support their beliefs or serve their interests.

The best way to make decisions based on good quality information, and filter out poor quality information, is to focus on facts and truth. The problem of what is good quality information harkens back to the philosophical Socratic question: What is the truth? Is the truth something you see with your own eyes (e.g., I'll believe it when I see it)? Or is the truth a fact that exists in a book? A Scientist may say that the truth can be discovered using empirical techniques, using a systematic process of testing, collecting evidence, and validation, and ideally in a controlled environment. A trained researcher would call this primary research. But since you cannot research everything yourself, you may rely on other, secondary sources, for information, like a reputable subject matter expert, or an accepted authority, who has already done much of that work for you. And by using a secondary source, you are able to collect evidence, test and validate your own knowledge, and improve the quality of the information your decisions are based on.

Relying on objective data and facts, rather than intuition, can improve quality of information. One way of doing that is by reducing decisions down to numbers. In business, for example, managers reduce much of a business's operations down to numbers, like business transactions, assets, expenditures, materials, labor, and overhead costs, to make sound, data driven, business decisions. If you only used intuition to make guesses, you really have no idea whether you were making a sound decision or a costly mistake that could bankrupt the business. For example, if you manage a business and do not factor in regular expenses, like land, labor, and production costs, you could be operating at a loss and not know it. A store owner who has shelves full of goods that never sell, loses the opportunity to make a profit on merchandise that could be sitting on those shelves. Reducing this information down to numbers can make these decisions easier and more intuitive.

5

Expertise

Abraham Maslow once wrote that "sufficient knowledge" enables people to solve problems and helps them in their moral and ethical choices when deciding their next course of action. As people become more knowledgeable, their choices and solutions become easier and more automatic. Knowledge, he said, "brings certainty of decision, action, choice and what to do." Even in opening the abdomen, the surgeon knows to remove the inflamed appendix before it bursts and kills the patient. This, he says, is "an example of truth dictating what must be done."[41] The result of having sufficient knowledge, or sufficient problem-solving skills, is that people are able to proceed with life confidently because they know what to do, and are able to figure out our next course of action. If you lack sufficient knowledge, you could rely on an expert who has already done that work for you.

A basic critical thinking skill is getting the facts you need to know what you are talking about. You simply cannot know what you are doing, if you do not know what you are talking about. And that is especially true for any subject that has a significant learning curve and requires knowhow. The more you know about a subject, the more capable you will be at making predictions about the consequences of decisions, and making decisions that lead to wanted outcomes. Many professionals have learned to use tools and techniques for reducing uncertainty when making costly decisions. A structural engineer, for example, who has special training may identify structural deficiencies the average person would overlook. Finance experts have many mathematical models for calculating the risks associated with investment decisions, reducing uncertainty about investment decisions, and potentially reducing investment mistakes and financial losses.

Knowhow is one of the most time and effort saving factors in decision-making. If you know how to do something, or be successful at something, then you should always be successful. A person who has already achieved success, knows the factors required to be successful, and may be more capable of repeating that success. The acquisition of knowhow, in terms of what makes a project successful or causes it to fail, can improve chances of success. This is why managers, usually, do not run successful businesses because of luck. And engineers do not build successful projects because they stumble upon the solution accidently. Having the knowhow to achieve success will improve your chances of success.

Alternatively, you can seek the advice or services of an expert, instead of wasting time and effort learning from trial-and-error mistakes. Experts can make choices easier by simplifying them down to a few simple choices. For example, a seven-page wine menu is overwhelming to a person who is not an expert. All of that information must be processed and researched to reduce uncertainty when trying to make the best choice. Having an overwhelming number of options may cause you to make a random choice, which may be a terrible choice. Or you may give-up and make no choice at all. The wine expert, on the other hand, should be able to provide advice about different wines, their sweetness, the foods they complement, and the best vintages to help you make the best choice. You could also download one of dozens of wine apps to your mobile device, to help you narrow down the right wine, assuming the app is unbiased and not sponsored by a wine producer who is trying to promote their brand of wine.

The ability to simplify complexity and make choices easier and more intuitive can significantly reduce serious errors. In business, some of that task is being automated using software, like Business Intelligence (BI) systems, to make complex datasets, and complex decisions, simpler and more intuitive. BI software does that by providing a dashboard that displays simple charts to illustrate and summarize production, expenses, revenues, and other factors of production, so that executives and managers can respond to business needs and make complex decisions easier and more automatic.

## 6
## Scenario Analysis

*Scenario analysis* is a critical thinking skill that involves modelling possible scenarios and making predictions about consequences. Seeing the potential consequences of implementing a solution can help you identify key success factors, like time or money, that would cause your project to fail.

Suppose you are a Director of Information Technology at a large corporation. If you understand how your technology systems work, then you are aware of how and why problems could arise, like system failures, cybercriminals, developer mistakes, a lack of systems monitoring, or hardware failures. Any of these scenarios creates uncertainty about potential downtime, lost revenue, lost customers, exposed personal information, or exposed intellectual property. And those problems may be prevented or mitigated by doing research, hiring experts, and testing scenarios. Suppose one day your database is held for ransom by cybercriminals. If that database is backed-up, and you have tested your backups, you should be able to quickly and easily recover your data and get running again. That is because you have considered and prepared for that scenario, maybe as a result of training or previous experience. But if you do not consider that scenario, or do not take the threat seriously, the consequences could be catastrophic to the business.

Scenario analysis can be especially useful in your personal and professional life. Thinking about possible scenarios in your relationships, employment, and financial situation, can enable you to prepare for potential problems. Everyone hopes they will never be the victim of a crime, or that they will never lose their job. But if you are prepared for those scenarios, you can more effectively mitigate potential losses. For example, if you are remodeling your living space, you could easily predict what could go wrong beforehand. You could imagine possible scenarios that would cause your project to fail or cause set-backs, budget overruns, or unnecessary accidents. And that scenario analysis would help you to determine the viability of the project before you start, foresee problems beforehand, and take measures to prevent those problems from occurring, to reduce the chances of encountering unexpected problems that would cause the project to fail.

## 7
## Reality Testing

A *reality test* is a critical thinking skill that allows you to prove or disprove the viability of an idea and whether it could actually work in reality. The Scientific Method follows a similar pattern. The Scientist starts with an unproven model (i.e., a hypothesis), and reality tests that hypothesis to see if the model is correct. You could also do that by building scale models or prototypes to see if your ideas work in reality. If they do, then you know your ideas will work as expected. Those tests will not only help you to test the viability of your idea, but to discover problems and missing features, learn from trial-and-error, and further research and develop the idea.

Some mental models are easier to validate than others. If you can quantify a model by measuring time, physical dimensions, or costs, it is easier to work with and validate. Determining whether a quantity is within a budgeted amount of time or money is easier to confirm than making guesses.

Models that are not easily numerically validated, like an idea intended to evoke emotion, can present greater uncertainty. For example, performing before an audience who judges and provides social validation. Since your stage performance depends on the opinions of the audience, you cannot consider yourself a great stage performer if no one else agrees with you. That is an example of testing your performance to make sure it delivers the intended result.

Reality tests not only reduce uncertainty in decision-making, they enable you to make informed life choices by revealing details that you could never consider otherwise. For instance, if you accept a job in an unfamiliar city, you may want to live close to your job. But if you follow that mental logic without reality testing your idea, you may end up in a living in a part of town you are unhappy with because it has a high crime-rate, noise pollution, or air pollution. So, you could reality test your choice by visiting the area, discussing the issue with a coworker or Realter, or doing online research.

8
Stages of Validation

In this section, we look at an example of how to reality test an idea. This section is not meant to serve as a best practice or standard method, only as an example of what that process may look like. The three stages of validation presented in this section are 1) question the model, 2) research the model, and 3) test the model.

*Stage 1: Question the model.*

Suppose you want to remodel your living space to make it more comfortable and inviting to guests. You start with a mental model of what you want to do. Since your model may not be perfect, you could start by brainstorming, whiteboarding the idea with other people, or ask people for their ideas or advice. This stage helps you consider the strengths and weaknesses of your idea, identify problems, and identify areas of improvement, based on what you and others already know.

Writing down the idea, creating a graphical representation, or creating a diagram, can help you and other people to visualize and study your model for problems. You can use this graphical model to consider possible scenarios, make predictions, and evaluate alternative possibilities. As you question your model and brainstorm ideas, you will get a better sense of whether the idea is even feasible and worth continuing before you invest a significant amount of time and money in creating something that may not work.

CRITICAL SKILLS FOR LIFE AND LEADERSHIP

*Stage 2: Research the model.*

When you first create your model, you are probably making assumptions about the availability of materials, like paint, colors, fabrics, and maybe furniture. To further reduce uncertainty about your plans, you need to research the unknowns about the project, and answer key questions that could cause the project to fail. For example, you have to research things, like the availability of paint colors, wall decorations, sizes and dimensions, and pricing, to make sure it is viable and fits within your budget. You may want to research different products, read reviews, and seek advice. Doing your homework and looking at other people's work, will enable you to learn what they have learned from their experiences and mistakes, so you do not repeat the same mistakes.

A simpler approach to solving this problem is to hire a specialist or expert who is already over the learning curve and solved those problems for you. For example, you could hire an interior designer who has done the homework, in terms of learning from experience, trial-and-error, and formal training, to propose a living space that you find desirable at a reasonable price. That would prevent you from wasting a considerable amount of valuable time and effort.

*Stage 3: Test the model.*

Once you have researched your idea, reality test your idea before creating the final solution. The importance of doing this is to ensure your solution works the way you predict. By reality testing your idea and doing a scaled-down model, you can find mistakes and failures before you blow your budget on a solution that may not work. You could, for example, break-down and test each individual part of the project, each color, and each piece of furniture, to make sure it works as expected. By reality testing your model, you avoid leaving too much up to the imagination and wishful thinking, which is more likely to cause your project to fail than succeed.

# CHAPTER IV:
# MOTIVATION

A prominent area of research among behavioral scientists involves trying to discover human motivations and human drives. The ability to interpret other people's motivations is, by itself, a basic personal skill that develops and evolves throughout life. People who lack that ability are more likely to misinterpret behavior or read too much into it, which leads to misunderstandings and unnecessary conflict. Understanding human motivation can also be instrumental in your life roles where you are trying to influence people, for example, as a leader, a parent, or instructor. In this chapter, we primarily focus on human motivation, and the problems of motivation. But in the next chapter, we look, in greater detail, at the motivational skills that can improve your success when trying to influence people.

1
Theories of Motivation

Over the years, many competing theories of motivation have emerged from many different academic disciplines. And some motivational techniques appear to be highly successful in practice. For instance, Marketers regularly try to influence buyers to purchase specific goods or services. And if those Marketers are successfully at changing people's buyer behavior, then what is their secret?

One of the more popular theories is Abraham Maslow's Hierarchy of Needs, published during the 1940's in a Theory of Human Motivation. His theory suggests that when basic needs are met, like physiological needs, or the need for food and safety, a person can move on to higher needs for things like belonging and personal acceptance. This theory is useful for explaining family dynamics at home, or social dynamics at work, to understand decision-making in the context of feeling safe and secure, or feeling threatened. When a person feels safe, that person may want to stay, bond, and form close relationships. But if that person feels threatened, that person may be more resistant to forming close relationships and may want to leave. The problem with this theory, as a general theory of motivation, is that it only applies to specific situations. It would not apply to explaining why Mahatma Gandhi, for example, went on a hunger strike to protest policy and fighting in India, which upends the hierarchy because it suggests that political needs outweigh the need for food and existence.

Another popular theory among Behaviorists, and Political and Economic theorists, is the idea that behavior is motivated by incentives, like rewards and punishments. People are averse to pain and discomfort and try to avoid it, and prefer the rewarding pleasures of consumption over pain. And certainly, many controlled laboratory experiments on pleasure seeking lab rats appear to confirm these conclusions. When you look at the human world, you can easily observe people seeking the rewards of income and an improved standard of living, the indulgences of pleasurable activities, in addition to avoiding punishment and condemnation by obeying laws and seeking social approval. All of these examples point to human behavior as, undeniably, being motivated by incentives.

The problem with this conclusion is that people are constantly surrounded by things that could reward them with pleasure they do not pursue. Businesses offer incentives to make purchases at discounts that buyers do not take advantage of. At any moment, a person could spend money on entertainment, but instead decides to work. And as people pursue their life interests, their goals may not even produce a financial reward, or the reward of happiness but, instead, may result in sacrifice and suffering. For example, risking one's life to help other people may not yield an immediate emotional or psychological reward. But, instead, it may be viewed as the right, or humane, thing to do.

Behavior is, without a doubt, goal-oriented, and people are motivated by end results, but not necessarily specific rewards or punishments. If all behavior were motivated by incentives, then you would never have to worry about an employee quitting so long as that worker's labor was sufficiently compensated. But people quit high-paying jobs for many reasons, maybe their boss is a jerk, or because they want to spend more time doing what they want. Each decision is made in the context of different circumstances with different people who have different interests and, therefore, different motives.

Human behavior is highly goal-oriented in that people are naturally motivated to satisfy biological and social needs for nourishment, safety, and income. So, you could conclude that people are primarily motivated to pursue their biological, social, or other personal goals. In fact, goals are often used to motivate worker performance and productivity within organizations. According to Management and Organizational Psychologist Dr. Edwin Locke's Goal Setting Theory of Motivation, when managers set clear and obtainable goals, worker productivity and performance increases. According to Dr. Locke, those goals should be slightly challenging to make the effort worth-while, but not so difficult that it leads to discouragement, giving-up, and failure.

Goal setting is motivational because it gives workers a course of action and an end result to work toward so workers know where to focus their energy. When workers lack clear and obtainable goals, they are less certain about what they should do, and are more likely to be idle and unproductive, or doing something they should not. The problem with Goal Setting Theory, as a general theory of human motivation, is that people may not, individually, be motivated by any clear, specific, rational, or realistic goals, even while they are motivated to obtain more of what they want.

Another prominent theory of motivation is Rational Choice Theory, which views people as motivated by self-interest. This theory presumes that when people are rational actors, they make choices that benefit their self-interest and avoid choices that do not. In Economic models, this theory is used to predict the choice a rational buyer or seller would make in a given scenario, which tends to be the choice that yields the most financial gain. That economic model can be used by a business owner to price goods and services, maximize profit, and determine whether a product is even viable, based on whether enough demand exists in the market at a given price.

Rational choice theory works well if we assume that all people are rational actors, and only make decisions that serve their self-interests. But when applied to general Psychology, the Rational Choice Theory falls short. People have biases and make decisions based on emotions, beliefs, and inaccurate or incomplete information, rather than objective reason. People have mental conditions that result in irrational decisions, like mental disorders, low self-confidence, low self-esteem, or self-destructive behaviors. So, for any theory of motivation to be truly universal, and applicable across a variety of disciplines, it needs to account even for the irrational side of human nature and the fact that people do not always act in their best interests.

## 2
## The Private Interest Theory of Motivation

My theory of motivation created for this book is the *Private Interest Theory of Motivation*, which suggests that people are motivated by the subject of interest, or object of interest, they attend to in the moment. This does not presume to fully know, or explain, people's motives. Instead, it explains each person's decisions as motivated by unique and complex factors that may be biological, social, emotional, or even irrational. This theory abstracts away some of the circumstantial details involved with motivation to explain more complex topics, like value creation, or why people perceive unfairness and injustice, both of which are topics of later sections in this chapter.

On a lower biological level, your brain is constantly scanning the environment for threats and opportunities, and giving attention to things that could threaten losses or present an opportunity to make gains, in terms of the things you want. That can motivate you to pursue, protect, and defend your interests, which could include physical safety, family, career, nation, or a cause.

Just as people have needs for their existence, like food, safety, and reproduction, they also have wants, in terms of the best, or most sufficient, option among the alternatives. People can always think of a better, and more desirable, option to pursue when trying to satisfy their needs. For example, if you were alone in the forest and need food to survive, you have many options to choose from, including certain types of plants. You could live under the forest canopy, build a shelter, or live in a cave. Among these alternatives, you probably want the best, or most convenient, option. Even after you select the best choice, you may continue seeking better options. And your opinion about what is better is privately known only to you. So, your motives, and what you really want, cannot be truly known or understood by anyone else.

The pursuit of private interest is sometimes viewed as a cynical and selfish pursuit. Sometimes people act in their own interests without considering how their decisions can have a negative impact on other people's lives. But to get more of what you want, in terms of a family, income, and help, you depend on the cooperation of other people. In fact, the pursuit of private interests may be entirely selfless and altruistic, like serving and protecting other people and contributing to the greater good, since people have shared interests and are willing to cooperate in pursuit of those interests. You can observe that when people form intimate relationships, work for employers, or volunteer for community activities.

## 3
## Self-Serving Biases

A *self-serving bias* is a tendency to favor one's own viewpoint over the viewpoints of other people. And often, those stubborn biases do not lead to be the best outcome for everyone. Consider, for example, during the turn of 20th century, two famous inventors, Thomas Edison and Nikola Tesla, had a feud over whether direct-current (DC) power or alternating-current (AC) power was the better solution. Edison believed that DC power was the better option for building a power grid. The problem with Edison's solution was that DC power stations were far less efficient and more expensive to maintain than AC power stations that could transmit power over much longer distances. Despite the disadvantages and limitations of DC power, Edison made it his mission to show how dangerous AC power was. In one publicity stunt, he electrocuted an Elephant to death, which inspired the electric chair designed to execute prisoners on death row. But eventually, Tesla's AC power station won-out and became the standard for the modern power grid.

Edison was stubborn in favoring his DC power over AC power because he had already arrived at a biased conclusion on the matter and was unwilling to consider alternative viewpoints. Political elections are overflowing with these types of self-serving biases, where candidates regularly argue that the truth is on their side, and that they, rather than their opponents, have the best solution.

Self-serving biases also come in the form of taking credit for one's successes and avoiding blame for failures. For example, a student who does well on a test may take full credit for the success. But as soon as he fails, suddenly the instructor is to blame for making the exam too difficult, or for putting tricky questions on the exam, or for not doing enough to prepare students for the exam.

Self-serving biases can lead to, what Psychologists call, the *endowment effect*, where a person's own possessions, abilities, and ideas are valued more than those of other people. Certainly, your possessions are valuable to you, and you may be motivated to protect and defend your possessions. But that can cause errors in thinking when you begin to overprice your possessions or overrate your abilities or ideas. Consequently, you may devalue and disregard the ideas, or decisions, of other people. And that can cause you to view your own behavior as more rational than other's. For example, Susan knows that she gets angry for good reasons. But as soon as Tim gets angry, Susan knows that Tim is a little crazy and has anger issues.

4
Self-Defeating Interests

*Self-defeating interests* are those that motivate people to act against their best interests. This idea goes to the core of why traditional theories of motivation fail. Contrary to what many motivational theories would say, people are not always rational and predictable and, instead, act on biases, emotions, poor habits, and personal beliefs.

Immediate interests, and what people attend to in the moment, like responding to biological urges or circumstantial events, drives human behavior more so than life goals or distant future outcomes. And so, people are susceptible to, what a Behavioral Scientist would call, temporal discounting, or time discounting, in which they place higher value on what they have now, and less value on what they could have in the future. For instance, Adam makes it a goal to exercise and eat healthy. But at the moment, he is sitting on the couch, eating potato chips, and watching television, which is far easier and more relaxing than doing the work of physical exercise. After all, he always has more time in the future to get healthy.

Life is lived in the moment. And even when people are fully capable of thinking strategically and considering longer-term consequences, they are easily distractible and lose cognitive focus when pursuing longer-term goals. Adam may want to learn a new language but complains he does not have time because he is too busy laying on the couch and watching television. Or maybe he spends too much money on an unnecessary item while paying down a debt. Or he overindulges in a three-course meal while on a weight-loss program. He wants to satisfy his urges in the moment, focusing on what is in front of his face, rather than on his longer-term aspirations.

Emotions are particularly notorious for dominating people's attention in the moment and motivating them to act against their best interests. For example, if Adam is angry at something his boss did at work today, then during his drive home, he may drive more aggressively than normal and become frustrated with slow drivers. These types of distressing circumstances can cause people to overreact and make poor decisions.

People also develop unhealthy or harmful interests, like obsessions or fixations. For example, people become addicted to activities, like gambling or illicit drugs. An average person may gamble, or have a drink, and maintain full control over one's desire for those things. But a person who is addicted may be preoccupied with anticipating the reward of the experience. That person may, then, seek to increase the frequency of engaging in those activities. And that increased frequency not only puts one at a greater risk of addiction, it increases the risk of experiencing negative consequences associated with the addiction, like unwanted behavioral, financial, or legal consequences.

## 5
## Value Creation

In a market economy, if you want something, you usually barter or exchange money for the item. The more you want it, the more money you are motivated to spend. This is how value is created. And the creation of value does not just apply to things sold in a market, but to personal and cultural values. The more you want something, the more you may be willing to sacrifice for it, in terms of time, money, and labor to obtain it. We could call this the Principle of Value Appreciation. And people are willing to risk their lives for things they want, and value, like family, or a cause they believe in.

Monetary exchange value, or trade value, is one of the more recognizable forms of economic value. The main reason money, itself, has value, is that it enables people to get more of what they want. In capital markets, value is created when a producer makes a good or service that is desirable and wanted enough, that people are willing to part with their hard-earned money to obtain it. And value can be added to an existing good or service to increase the demand for the product. For example, a person may purchase an old piece furniture, put work into it, and make it desirable enough so that someone would be willing to purchase it at a higher price.

Producers need to put enough work into their goods or services, and add enough value, for people to want to buy them. Otherwise, you could create the product yourself, and it would have little, or no, value to you. You could do-it-yourself (DIY) many things, but not things that require a significant amount of expertise or difficulty. And, therefore, when demand for those items exists in the marketplace, they tend to have greater value.

*Human capital* is another valued asset that includes knowledge and skills that have monetary exchange value. In a knowledge-based or skills-based industry that requires expertise, skills are what employers pay for. So, it may be possible to add value to your services by developing your knowledge and skillset, but only if the buyers recognize the value you bring. In a similar way, managers are able to appreciate the value of their workforce by testing, or encouraging, workers to develop their knowledge and skillsets to become more fit in performing their job roles. Improving the talent in a business's workforce can increase the value of the business and its product offering as a result of improved operational effectiveness and improved efficiencies, which improves functionality and reduces unnecessary costs.

*Personal* or *cultural value* usually consists of things, including material artifacts, like family heirlooms or sports memorabilia, or traditions, like holidays and birthdays. In terms of personal values, people have different opinions about the value of things. For example, a person who collects small plastic figurines may place greater value on them, especially if they are valued among collectors, than someone who would never buy those items. Or a person wanting to purchase a million-dollar artwork that other people find ugly, may be interested in appealing to a certain class of people, or maybe it makes a statement about one's values, or the owner wants to possess something that is rare, or wants the best that the world has to offer. Or the artwork may simply be an investment, and a way to diversify one's portfolio of assets by putting money into a security that is expected to appreciate in value.

6
The Effect of Gains & Losses

Earlier we looked at how people are motivated by private interest, specifically to make wanted gains or avoid un-wanted losses in terms of those private interests. And much of that motivation stems directly from, what I call, the *effect of gains and losses*, which is the influence the perception of gains or losses has on a person's mental state, emotions, and behavior. On a biological level, people are motivated to pur-sue opportunities to make gains, in terms of security, nour-ishment, help, or anything that leads to growth and devel-opment. And people are motivated to protect themselves from the threat of losses, in terms of food, safety, help, or any resources that would result in physical decline, weak-ness, or death. For example, if Bill does not want to lose his job, he will probably try harder to keep it. That behavior is motivated by the prospect of experiencing an unwanted employment loss.

Looking at the consequences of decisions as gains or losses, can be more practical than framing them as rewards and punishments. They are similar because when a person gains something, the reward centers in the brain light-up and release pleasurable hormones. Or you may try to avoid unwanted loss that could result in disappointment or re-gret. People are willing to endure pain, which is commonly associated with punishment, and are willing to avoid pleasures, which are ubiquitous in developed societies, to make wanted gains or avoid unwanted losses. So, the prospect of experiencing gains or losses is far more motivating than simple rewards and punishments.

The effect of gains and losses also enables people to distinguish between good decisions and poor decisions. Intuitively, we could say that a "good" or "rational" decision is one that make's a person better-off. And that is exactly what is taught in the School of Business where students learn that a good decision is one that makes both the buyer and seller better off. In this "win-win" situation, the buyer gets the desired good or service and the seller gets the desired compensation. So, anytime a person makes a decision that benefits everyone involved, it's a good decision. In contrast, when a person gains at the expense of other people, or causes a person to experience an unfair loss, like in the crime of theft, it's usually judged to be an injustice. This, of course, is not true for every organization, including national defense, law enforcement, or criminal justice, where the objectives do not always seek win-win outcomes.

People's private motivations create another layer of complexity to decision-making. People tend to consider a good decision as one that serves their interests. And when a decision results in devastating or catastrophic losses, most people would say that was a poor decision. But suppose Jim is seeking spiritual enlightenment and forgoes financial opportunities to obtain that enlightenment. In his mind, he is making the best decision for him. But Sara, who is desperately seeking more financial opportunities, thinks that Jim is making an unwise decision. Consequently, Sara does not trust Jim's judgment. So, whether a decision is perceived to be good or rational is completely relative to that person's unique interests, ambitions, and life goals.

In other words, the effect of gains and losses, is relative to a person's private interests. People tend to judge the quality of decisions, and whether a decision is "good" and "rational," based primarily on their own wants and interests, and whether they make gains or experience losses in terms of their interests. So, receiving an unwanted thing, may not be perceived to be a gain. And losing an unwanted thing, may not be perceived as a loss. It all really depends on a person's unique interests.

Research by Psychologists Daniel Kahneman and Amos Tversky found that people tend to be loss averse, and avoid loss more than the prospect of gains. If you are uncertain about whether a decision will lead to a positive gain or a negative loss, you may cautiously avoid it all together to avoid the loss. Intuitively, this makes sense because you cannot be certain about what you gain, but you can be certain about what you lose. So, you protect yourself by proceeding with caution, to avoid costly mistakes.

In practice, avoiding unwanted losses is not possible since making gains, in terms of what you want, requires the expenditure of time, money, and opportunities. Those losses are not necessarily the result of poor decisions, or a decision you should regret, since those losses were made when you were striving to gain more of what you want. An Economist would call that a sunk cost, which is a loss that you are not able to get back and should not regret.

The effect of gains and losses also has a dynamic influence on personal relationships. Significant losses, like unemployment, divorce, gaining or losing personal help, losing personal acceptance, and disagreements in which a person losses support for an idea, can all have a dramatic effect on people. In fact, these events sometimes have such a dramatic effect that people will desperately lie to avoid rejection, or become emotional when they occur.

## 7
## Emotional Consequences

The effect of gains and losses has a tremendous emotional influence on human behavior. You can observe this when a person wins a game, receives social approval, lands a new job, or gets married. All of these evoke joy and happiness. Losses, on the other hand, like losing a game, social disapproval, employment termination, or having something stolen from you, can evoke anger or sadness, or hurtful feelings.

In terms of lower, instinctual, abilities, people have warning systems (e.g., fear), or biological defenses (e.g., anger), that serve to protect them from losses to their physical safety, personal relationships, or financial status. Usually these systems are helpful, like when fear protects you from losing life and limb in a horrible accident. Or a person's stress levels may increase at the prospect of not completing a project on time. But other times, fear can override reason and cause people to behave irrationally, like when a motorist is late for work and drives at unsafe speeds, putting oneself and other motorists at risk.

Even the smallest things can influence a person's happiness throughout the day. A few years ago, a colleague of mine began celebrating because he won some virtual coins while playing a video game on his mobile phone. The coins had no use or monetary value. But he was ecstatic and celebrating because he was a winner. This same excitement occurs among fans at sports events. The fans of the winning team celebrate and jump with joy while the fans of the losing team are shocked, horrified, and emotionally crushed as they watch their team's demise. At the Euro 2016 Championship, rivalry between Russian and English football fans was so intense and so emotionally charged that police resorted to firing tear gas into the crowds and made arrests to stop the fighting in the streets.[60]

The effect of gains and losses also has a significant role in motivating productivity. If Lauren imagines that she will be happy once her career reaches a certain income, it may push her to strive harder. She may be further motivated to work long hours, save money, or spend her time wisely, if she imagines the unhappiness she will experience if she lives without those things.

According to a Pew Research Center survey, people with more education, income, and household goods, experienced greater satisfaction than people without those things. The survey looked at whether the participants had specific household goods, like a "television, refrigerator, washing machine, microwave oven, computer, car, bicycle, motorcycle/scooter and radio." Many of these, like the car or washing machine, are conveniences that reduce the burden and workload of living, which enables people to spend more time enjoying life. The greater number of items the participants possessed, the greater amount of happiness they reported experiencing. But the participants also said that some things were more important than financial prosperity, like "health, their children's education and being safe from crime."[50]

The problem with the pursuit of material wealth is that it comes at a price. When people work longer hours, and more of their time, labor, and attention is demanded by clients or employers, it increases unhealthy stress levels and can lead to unhealthy lifestyle habits. Married couples who place a high value on financial gains may start arguments and conflicts over financial concerns and potential losses. They may blame each other or harbor resentment for financial losses. And those feelings could lead to more conflicts that increase stress levels and put a strain on the relationship. So, the pursuit of material wealth alone may not necessarily lead to happiness.

In fact, according to a study by Ryan Howell at San Francisco State University and Thomas Gilovich at Cornell University, people are happier when they spend their money on experiences that make them happy, like playing games or going to sports events, rather than tangible objects. The happiness gained from a possession fades over time, while the happiness from an experience may be recalled any number of times. Happy experiences may also include family and friends, and can be shared with other people in conversations or social media. Gilovich suggested that this is reason policy makers should consider creating more public works projects designed to provide citizens with opportunities for positive experiences in the community.[34]

If we looked to Nature for wisdom and guidance on happiness, as the Ancient philosophers did, it would teach us that all human life, like all other life forms, operates on a continuum of progress. You never fully reach a constant state of happiness. Instead, happiness, like all other human appetites, is insatiable. Once it is satisfied, it grows hungry again. And since happiness is a temporary and fleeting emotion, it could never be a final end but, instead, an ongoing effort that requires work and perseverance.

In other words, happiness is an emotion that comes from within, rather than from an external source. That's why money does not buy happiness. If you want to be happy, you need to nourish and feed that happiness, by doing things that make you happy, by enjoying life, playing games, or creating happy experiences. Happiness can also come from work and effort, when you benefit from the fruits of your labor. If you have things in your life you are dissatisfied with, you can set goals, and work to change those things, to make life more satisfying.

8

Fairness

Fairness, or equity, may be defined as having equal opportunities and equal treatment, which is directly related to the effect of gains and losses. To understand why, put two children together and give one a toy. With many children, the child who did not receive a toy may see it as unfair because the two children are being treated differently. When teenagers see their friends receiving privileges, like the ability to stay out late, or permission to attend an event, they may sense this "unfairness" when they are denied the same privileges.

In the adult world, this perception of fairness largely depends on what people agree to, in terms of what they gain and must give up, and whether they are satisfied with the outcome. The economic definition of a fair exchange is one in which both parties agree to the terms of the exchange. But when one person gains at the expense of the other, the victim did not agree to the loss, for example, a good or service that you paid for, but did not receive. That type of loss would be unfair because you gave a person money, but did not receive the product in exchange.

Cultural differences also exist in what people consider to be fair. For example, during the 1950s, a prevalent cultural norm among married couples in the United States was a gender-based division of labor where the wife stayed home and took care of the family, while the husband worked and earned an income. Today, with more access to birth control, women have more independence to pursue careers. And many women view the expectation to become a stay-at-home wife as an unfair loss of rights and opportunities.

This desire for fairness is a motivating factor and the primary reason for writing and enforcing agreements. If you work for an employer, you may have signed a document that provides yourself and your employer with protections about pay and the possession of company property to prevent either party from experiencing unacceptable losses. Or if you purchased an expensive piece of electronics, you may have purchased a warranty that guarantees replacement if the item is damaged within a certain amount of time. Or maybe you made an oral agreement with a neighbor that her teenage child will not be throwing loud and crazy parties at three o'clock in the morning. All of these agreements protect those involved from unfair losses, like the loss of sleep.

Other types of losses, for example, in standard of living (i.e., having material wealth) or quality of life (i.e., having safe food and water), can create unfavorable conditions that can influence the satisfaction of citizens. Some examples include urban decay, a crumbling infrastructure, pollution, a lack of employment, or crime, all of which can invoke a sense of loss to a person's safety, job opportunities, income, or the ability to commute. All of these influence a person's expectations about the future and the person's outlook on life. When citizens have opportunities to make gains, in terms of employment, business, protection, quality of life, job opportunities, transportation, or enjoyable activities, they have fewer reasons to be discontented with life in the community, and more opportunities to experience greater satisfaction.

9

Justice

Justice is an act of holding someone accountable for behavior that results in an unfair loss. For example, when a perpetrator causes a person to experience an unfair loss, like the loss of property, the loss of health and safety, or the loss of a loved one, the victims may want to get justice by preventing the perpetrator from repeating the offense. When people experience injustice and have no recourse, like when the criminal justice system fails them, or when unjust actions are protected by law, it creates a since of lawlessness where people are being unfairly harmed and have no protections. In those circumstances, victims may still want to prevent the offender from repeating the crime, but have no legal means to do so.

Even today, certain types of unjust actions are protected by law, for example, At-Will employment laws in states like Oklahoma, where employers are free to use and abuse privileges without being held accountable for their actions. A colleague of mine, who is a highly qualified and model employee, was fired for trying to report serious and very careless management abuses, many of which were criminal. Under the State At-Will employment laws, it's illegal to fire someone for filing an abuse report. But when he sought legal counsel, he was told by numerous wrongful termination Lawyers that they could not represent him. And it significantly damaged his career and financial situation as a result of recruiters and hiring managers not believing him.

The purpose of the criminal justice system is to be an intermediary to citizens, and provide them with law enforcement and civil services to maintain civil order by preventing revenge and retaliation crimes. Without legal services or a criminal justice system, people would be motivated to take justice into their own hands and strike back to prevent the perpetrator from repeating the offense. And historically, you can find many examples of these tit-for-tat, back-and-forth, battles that have perpetuated long-standing feuds between families, neighbors, and nations.

Other forms of injustice include unfair discrimination on the basis of race, ethnicity, sex, or other factors, which causes losses of freedoms, losses of employment opportunities, and losses of personal safety. When citizens of a community have greater protection from injustice, they tend to experience fewer instances of unfairness, fewer reasons to be discontented, and greater satisfaction with life in the community. Not having those protections, and not having the legal services to address injustices where people are being harmed by people with malicious intent, can lead to a state of dissatisfaction and discontent. So, creating policies that protect citizens from these types of losses, and allowing people to contribute equally, has shown to improve satisfaction and economic conditions, and reduced uncivilized strife, within the community.

# CHAPTER V:
# MOTIVATIONAL SKILLS

Motivational skills are skills or techniques for motivating people, which are essential skills in positions of influence, like leadership, parenting, instruction, friendships, and in many other life roles. In this chapter, we build on the last chapter to understand what techniques are effective when attempting to motivate people. If the motivational theory presented in the last chapter is correct, then not all traditional methods for motivating people will work, as we will see in the following section on incentive-based motivation.

## 1
## Incentive-Based Motivation

A popular theory among Political and Economic theorists is that behavior is motivated by incentives. Some examples include obeying the laws to avoid fines or jail time, working long hours to earn an income, or performing well academically to receive a high grade-point average. Without a doubt, people do respond to incentives when they are in the form of making wanted gains, or avoiding unwanted losses, in the context of their private interests. But they do not always respond to incentives when they are in the form of rewards and punishments.

In his book *Drive: The Surprising Truth About What Motivates Us*, Daniel Pink cites numerous examples of how people are motivated more by intrinsic rewards and the desire to do something, rather than extrinsic rewards and punishments, like money or the threat of imprisonment, as the Rational Choice Theory suggests.[51] According to Pink, people do not always have to be compensated to perform work. For example, software developers regularly make contributions to Open Source projects without any expectation of monetary compensation.

The reason Open Source projects are successful is not because people prefer to slavishly work for free, but because they have some intrinsic value to gain from it. People like to volunteer their time and labor to worthy causes where it is needed. And that gives them an opportunity to apply and develop their skills, demonstrate their talent, and gain valuable experience. That intrinsic motivation, Pink says, has contributed to the rise of Wikipedia and the decline of traditional for-profit encyclopedias. Open Source software projects do, of course, provide other practical benefits, like not wasting needless time rewriting code. If a developer finds a bug, security vulnerability, or missing feature, in a project they use, they can submit a fix to the developer, or fork the project all together.

Pink cites a number of studies that show how increasing incentives, like monetary compensation, does not always increase the quality or quantity of work performed. And in some cases, the quality actually decreases, like when a person takes shortcuts to achieve goals, or when a person is corrupted by the anticipation of increasing rewards. For instance, if management offers a bonus for filling a sales quota, sales associates may do whatever is necessary, including lying to potential buyers, to make sales.

Rewarding specific behaviors also primes people to only perform work when a reward is provided. If a parent pays a child to perform a chore, like taking out the garbage, that child may stop performing the chore when no payment is made. Despite the fact that people are motivated by rewards and punishments, Pink argues, they are motivated by much more than the incentives proposed by Rational Choice Theory.

This intrinsic motivation that Pink writes about is unmistakably the pursuit of private interest. If a child stops taking out the garbage due to a lack of payment, it's because the compensation itself became the goal, rather than maintaining a clean home. Passion drives productivity and quality. But without interest, passion does not exist. This is why so many fully capable grade-school students fail. The extrinsic motivators of grades or scholarship are not enough to make them interested in the curriculum. If they were genuinely interested, they would voluntarily do it without being told, similar to a health-conscious person who enjoys a morning jog, or a historian who is genuinely intrigued about revealing the mysteries of human history, or a technology enthusiast who is fascinated by the new capabilities that could be discovered while playing with robotics. An instructor may be able to spark the student's interests, not just by making it fun or giving good grades, but by showing the student how it is useful and beneficial.

So, incentives, like money, are not enough to motivate behavior. People are not motivated to do anything for money. If they were, any man should be able to walk up to any woman, and propose sex for money. If we applied a rudimentary economic model to that scenario, both parties would certainly benefit and both would have something to gain by cooperating. But that's not how people think or operate. Certain decisions must be within their frame of interest and, specifically, in line with achieving specific life goals.

Understanding the role that interest plays is a useful management skill. When workers lose interest in their work, they lose motivation to be productive and make contributions, even when they are being sufficiently financially compensated. So, effectively motivating a team, and increasing their productivity and performance, may involve developing interest and pride in producing higher quality work, gaining beneficial skills and experience, gaining opportunities for advancement, or achieving organizational goals.

## 2
## Marketing

So far, we have learned that to be an effective influencer, you have to appeal to people's private interests. You could, for example, show a person why making one choice over another is in one's best interests, which may motivate a person to voluntarily do it. In fact, this is exactly how marketers influence buying behaviors in practice. They attempt to show potential buyers why they would be better off buying their product. And if marketers are able to change and influence behavior, and motivate people to make different choices, then certainly those techniques could be applied to other applications. So, the remainder of this section looks at some techniques used by Marketers for doing that.

The first of those is to know your target audience and, more specifically, to know their interests. Marketers do that by dividing populations into demographic segments or, in other words, by grouping people together based on similar interests. People of a certain age, for example, are going to be interested in certain products. Children are going to be interested in toys, new parents are going to be interested in diapers, and retired adults will be interested in retirement communities. Marketers collect this demographic information from people's web browsing and purchase history, ultimately to reduce unnecessary waste and annoyance by marketing only to people who are likely to buy the product.

Effectively influencing people also requires controlling attention. Without the ability to gain and control attention, Marketers have no influence over buyer decisions or the ability to change buyer habits. In fact, the whole purpose of advertisement is to divert people's attention away from what they are doing to show them why they want a product. A strategy Marketers have used, in recent years, is to create a viral advertisement that is so interesting, entertaining, or unbelievable that it is redistributed and shared among a target demographic. If you can control people's attention, assuming you are not annoying them, then you can control what they attend to in the moment, and potentially what they want when they make a purchase.

Influencing and changing behavior also requires changing expectations, and changing people's predictions about certain choices. Those expectations may be based on past experiences, or what they read or imagine. For example, if you are told that a Restaurant's food is terrible and could give you food poisoning, it may influence your decision to dine there. People spend large sums of money on an expensive education, expecting to increase their expertise and income. And those expectations influence their productivity, work ethic, behavior, and personal sacrifices, as they pursue that expertise.

Sales people often try to change buyer expectations by overcoming buyer objections. Or, Marketers may attempt to demonstrate how a product makes life better, more entertaining, or improves health, security, or sex appeal. The product has to be good enough, and desirable enough, to be wanted, or it will fail. And only when the perceived value of the product is greater than the money sacrificed to purchase it, does it make since to buy the item.

How the product makes people feel can influence buyer expectations, which is a tactic known as emotional branding. For instance, an actor in a car commercial may say that she is so happy and excited with her new car, its warranty, and how it drives, that it makes the viewers of that commercial want a similar experience. Or a restaurant commercial may show actors dining at the restaurant who are extremely delighted, laughing, and enjoying the food. Ads, like these, attempt to shape the viewers expectations about the experience they will have if they purchase the product.

Buyer expectations are strongly influenced by brand reputation. And according to Psychologists Amos Tversky and Daniel Kahneman, people tend to be loss averse, or cautious, in the brands the buy from. Intuitively this makes since because not knowing anything about a product puts you at greater risk of an unwanted purchase. So, to improve confidence in your purchase, you buy a brand you already know and are familiar with. This is why businesses often find a substantial barrier to entry when trying to bring a new product to market. The business has to show how their product is different, or better, than their competitors using a differentiation strategy.

Using these marketing strategies, you could formulate a strategy, or develop a program, for influencing and changing behavior. To do that, you may include tactics, like appealing to what your audience wants, keeping their focus and attention, influencing their expectations, having fun with the subject to evoke positive emotions, and showing your audience why a specific choice is the best choice. You could apply these techniques to giving a presentation, to managing a team, and to designing programs aimed at improving life skills.

3

Encouragement & Discouragement

Another way of influencing behavior is by providing encouragement or discouragement. This technique is especially effective when you are in a close personal relationship with the person you are trying to influence. This works especially well in life roles, like instruction, coaching, leadership, or parenting, in which you can have close contact with those you are trying to influence, to provide words of encouragement.

Encouragement, as the root of the word suggests, instills courage in a person or confidence in a person's abilities. When you encourage a wanted behavior, you are trying to further that behavior, or to develop new skills, like being a better expert or a stronger athlete. Encouragement takes many forms, including words of inspiration, being a cheerleader, and expressing trust and confidence in a person. When the feedback we receive from other people provides social validation, it can be encouraging and confirms that those behaviors are wanted and valued. And that encouragement can motivate a person to repeat and further develop those abilities.

Discouragement, on the other hand, causes a person to

lose confidence in one's abilities and is a demotivator of be-havior, which can have both positive or negative influences. For example, discouragement can positively influence be-havior when it prevents a person from engaging in harmful activities. But it can have a negative influence when people become discouraged with life in general as a result of expe-riencing significant adversity. When a person is constantly being treated poorly, continues to fail, and has low confi-dence in one's abilities, that person may be more likely to give-up. If a parent only punishes a child without providing any positive feedback or encouragement, or does not help the child do better, then the child would live in a constant state of discouragement and may feel worthless. It's easier to feel defeated and view life as an insurmountable prob-lem, when you are frequently reminded that you will never amount to anything.

The extent to which human development can be encour-aged partly depends on how receptive people are to encour-agement. Young children, for example, may not always be receptive to adult influences. During that time, parents usu-ally try to guide the child's development to keep the child safe, or help the child learn socially acceptable behaviors. But as the child grows older and develops a greater since of individuality, those attempts can conflict with the child's own interests. But encouraging a child to develop certain skills that can be beneficial in performing one's life roles, can be far more influential on the child's behavior than spending time together, social pressure, threats, or bribery. Or, as Emile Durkheim once put it, "the rule prescribing such behavior must be freely desired, that is to say, freely accepted; and this willing acceptance is nothing less than an enlightened assent."[19]

Role models, and learning from example, can provide

another form of encouragement whereby people learn the skills necessary to perform a role. Children may be especially reliant on role modelling when they have no other forms of guidance. During the 1960's, Social Learning theorists Albert Bandura, Dorothea Ross, and Sheila Ross, did a series of studies at Stanford University where they collected evidence for how aggressive and non-aggressive role models influence children's behavior. Children assigned the aggressive role models exhibited aggressive behaviors. And children assigned to non-aggressive role models, or no role model, exhibited fewer aggressive behaviors.[28] Their findings suggest that admirable role models may bring out admirable qualities in children, and unscrupulous role models may inspire children to perform unscrupulous acts. And for that reason, role modelling can be very beneficial when the child has a strong role model, but is a very limited and requires the aspect of luck.

Instead of relying entirely on role modelling, parents could also encourage their children to develop specific abilities, by encouraging them to solve problems that challenge and test their abilities. Some of those challenging activities may include activities that challenge the child's intellectual abilities, physical abilities, or social abilities, which furthers the development of personal skills, including communication, memory and problem solving, character and trust-building, or engaging in healthy activities. This desire to take on challenging problems can plant a seed of self-confidence that enables the child to grow into a confident and resilient adult capable of taking on the difficulties of living.

According to research by Psychologist Carol Dweck and others, self-confidence may influence personal and financial success far more than intelligence.[20] People who are confident in their abilities have the grit and tenacity to continue trying until the desired result is achieved. Self-confident children may have better mental resilience during difficult times, the ability to handle challenges, and a better outlook on life. Lacking self-confidence, in contrast, would be discouraging and could lead to despair and giving-up.

Within human organizations, the ability of management and leadership to provide encouragement can have a profound influence on organizational performance. For that reason, organizational cultures are sometimes built around words of encouragement. Or, an organization may encourage skills development by incentivizing training and education. Without certain types of skillsets, the performance of the organization suffers, or management needs to hire outside labor. But managers can encourage workers to develop or improve skillsets, in addition to improve their performance and productivity. When an organization has the right processes and skillsets, not only does the business operate more efficiently, it gets a better return on investment for its labor.

The reason why providing encouragement may work in human organizations has to do with two different types of effects: the Pygmalion effect; and the Galatea effect. The Pygmalion effect was originally described by Robert Rosenthal, PhD, during the 1960's, in which he suggested that expectations about how well a person will perform can influence that person's performance. In 1969, Dr. J. Sterling Livingston further suggested that the effect could be applied to management.[35] For example, when a manager has positive feelings and high expectations of subordinates, they are more likely to have high expectations of themselves. When a manager repeatedly expresses confidence in a subordinate's abilities, the subordinate may be encouraged by the manager's confidence and may be more likely to perform at a higher level.

Similarly, the Galatea effect suggests that how we feel about ourselves, and our confidence in our own abilities, influences our performance. If you know you are capable of something, you are more likely to do it. So, by giving people more freedom to develop their abilities and empower them to have more influence within the organization, managers may be able to increase worker's self-confidence to perform at a higher level.[27]

4

Commitment

Motivation within organizations can also be improved by increasing the commitment of members. Commitment refers to a person's devotion and dedication to something, like work, relationships, a career, a hobby, or a cause. Without enough commitment, goals are not achievable. Your commitment is demonstrated in what you are willing to do, in terms of the time and energy you spend to achieve personal or organizational goals. Commitment may also be used interchangeably with obligations, or agreements, when it refers to how you allocate your time on your schedule, like committing a time-slot to attending a dinner.

Goal-setting is one of the more basic motivational techniques that can increase commitment to a cause, or goal, because it provides you with a well-defined objective to strive for. According to goalsetting researcher Dr. Edwin Locke, setting clear and achievable goals gives workers a course of action and a place to focus their energy, which can increase their productivity and performance. When workers lack clear and achievable goals, they are more likely to be uncertain about what to do and more likely to be idle and unproductive. Goals should also be challenging enough to be worthwhile, but not so difficult that workers become discouraged and give-up.

Creating realistic obligations that you are able to following through with, and avoiding losing propositions, in terms of time, knowledge, and skillsets, can also be motivating. Behavioral Scientists sometimes call an increased commitment to a losing proposition an escalation of commitment, or the sunk-cost fallacy. For example, suppose a manager says to the Physicist: "We have already put millions of dollars into the development of our eternal youth device that we promised investors. We cannot let our investors down. We have to continue developing the technology until it works, whatever it takes." The manager, in this instance, is following the logic that projects fail only when an insufficient amount of time or energy is committed to their success. So, they continue developing the device, even if they are never able to prove that such a device could exist.

Financial incentives can also improve commitment, increase productivity, improve the quality of work, and retain workers, but only to a limited extent. In fact, in the business world, you will find countless examples of workers who are paid large sums of money, who quit their jobs to do something else. So, increasing commitment requires something more than financial incentives alone.

One of the more effective ways to increase commitment may be to improve job satisfaction or, more specifically, recognizing and eliminating the causes of dissatisfaction. A worker who is dissatisfied, or discontented, is more likely to quit. That is especially true if a worker dreads coming to work, is fearful of job security, suspicious of management, or has constant thoughts of quitting. Some possible reasons for dissatisfaction and demotivation is inadequate training, a lack of clearly defined goals or purpose, unfair treatment, or a lack of appreciation. Management can overcome each of these by exercising certain management skills, like providing training where necessary, communicating goals, policing unfair behavior, and showing appreciation. Each of these makes workers feel that their personal interests are protected, and motivates them to be more committed to the business and its objectives.

In 2012, Google conducted in internal study they called Project Aristotle to understand what makes the most productive and creative teams. And aside from the different personality types among team members, what made the biggest difference was that members were allowed to take risks and propose new ideas without judgment or criticism.[17] Since the study, people have referred to this technique as creating a "safe environment" in which members are safe from negative judgment and criticism, which allows workers to operate without feelings of insecurity that could cause workplace dissatisfaction.

Training programs can also improve job satisfaction when it improves worker's ability to perform their job better and advance their professional skillset, especially in knowledge-based occupations. Being a more highly skilled professional translates into being a more valuable asset to the business, which may boost a worker's self-esteem. A lack of trained workers, or a lack of sufficient skillsets, causes organizational performance to suffer. In technology, for example, that could literally mean down systems at the point-of-sale, slow development on projects, poor implementation, security vulnerabilities, all of which translates into dissatisfied clients, dissatisfied employees, and dissatisfied management.

Creating a fair workplace can improve job satisfaction. This means following standards for ethical behavior, and hiring and promoting skilled workers, to create a sense of trust and fairness. As soon as management is viewed as acting against the interests of employees, in some way, by breaching the implicit or explicit agreement that binds them in an employer and employee relationship, it may be viewed as unfair and may become a source of job dissatisfaction. Some examples may include being shamed or humiliated, or making sex a precondition for continued employment. If a sense of fairness is not enforced by management, it creates personal conflicts and job dissatisfaction, both of which are sources of further problems by causing a decline in performance, quality, and client service.

Additionally, unfairness could occur when an employer (i.e., the business owner or hiring manager) has ulterior motives. For instance, an employer who has difficulty finding an applicant for a specific job, may not disclose the true nature of the job during the interview. The employer may, then, use a bait-and-switch technique to assign an employee to a job that either goes beyond the scope of the initial employment agreement, or involves completely different work.

Declining commitment occurs for many reasons, including job dissatisfaction, personal conflicts, and conflicts of interest. When people disagree, or dislike, their coworkers, they may refuse to communicate or cooperate with them. That causes organizational dysfunction where workers are incapable of working together to achieve goals. And, consequently, those goals are never met. A conflict of interest, whereby a worker is putting one's own interests before the interests of the business or organization, is another cause of decline in commitment. A worker may be using the business's property for one's own personal objectives, like in the case of embezzlement. Or a manager may be making hiring or promotion decisions based on whether a candidate would threaten one's job security, as a result of being more qualified or the manager being less skilled for the role.

## 5
## Social Power

*Social power* is the ownership or control of resources, including the ability to control and motivate behavior. Commonly recognized forms of social power include organizational management, business owners, politicians, leaders of social causes, or wealthy people. These are people who are capable of influencing behavior as a result of payment in exchange for services, policy enforcement, threat or coercion, or charisma.

Most people have a normal, or average amount of, social power, which includes the ownership of property, influencing friends and family, or holding power in an organization to which they belong. Having control of your own behavior, by itself, gives you the power to further your own interests. But the drive to acquire more power may also mean relinquishing control to someone, like an employer, who pays for your labor and services, and provides you with the financing to do more.

Contrary to the popular quote by John Acton, "power tends to corrupt and absolute power corrupts absolutely," power, by itself, does not necessarily change a person's motives. Rather, power gives a person the ability to further one's own interests, whatever those interests may be. A criminal may have a very small amount of power and be absolutely corrupt. And a wealthy business owner, who has tremendous power over a workforce, and financial power to buy services for any purpose imaginable, may use that power to grow the business, employ more people, and philanthropically and give back to the community.

Power can be corrupting, depending on a person's motives. For example, a person who has a low opinion of others, may be more likely to treat them poorly when they do not have to answer for their decisions. And the world has a long history of people who are extremely powerful, some of whom have unlimited control over nations, who use their power for serving their own interests.

A person's power position refers to a person's superordinate or subordinate position within an organization. For example, in a family, the superordinate position would be the parent. In a business, it would be the business owner. And within a political organization, it would be the leader. And that power position determines who that person answers to, if anyone. The employee, in the subordinate position, depends on the employer for an income, not the other way around. And people who have power within organizations and financial independence have more potential to abuse their power and privileges and never face consequences.

People have different methods for gaining, and holding-on to, power. A person may gain, and maintain, power by threat or coercion as you see in a dictatorship type of structure. Controlling behavior by threat or coercion is often successful, but has the potential to negatively impact people who may want to put an end to the threat. But people also gain power by furthering other people's interests, as you see in a more democratic type structure. And people may be more willing to support and promote those who further and protect their interests.

Knowing the social dynamics underpinning social power, power positions, and how people gain and lose power, can help you make better decisions within a power structure. But that requires more than an understanding of power, by itself. It requires an understanding of how to further other people's interests, effectively use personal skills, in addition to many other topics discussed in this book.

# CHAPTER VI:
# RESPONSIBILITY

If you looked up responsibility in the dictionary, you would find a variety of definitions that include: Having a duty or obligation to fulfill; being accountable; having the ability to act independently; or being a source of blame. And in this chapter, we look at how responsibility is more than merely accepting attribution, like blame or credit, for a decision.

Responsibility is a legal concept. In the United States, for example, if someone is injured by your pet, you may be held legally responsible. When you mature into adulthood, you are considered legally responsible for your choices. Psychologists are sometimes called by a Court to testify whether a defendant could be legally responsible for actions that caused harm, or whether those actions were the result of a mental disability or mental disorder.

The concept of responsibility also applies to responsible living, responsible management, and responsible policy. For example, drinking responsibly means fully understanding the consequences of drinking alcohol. Since a brain impaired by alcohol is more likely to hurt people, or cause a motor vehicle accident, drinking responsibly takes into account those negative consequences and avoids them by preventing or restricting the consumption of alcohol. Anytime someone is making decisions that have predictable negative consequences on a regular basis, is not making responsible decisions.

Similarly, Lawmakers sometimes struggle with drafting responsible policy that accounts for all the consequences of a policy and its impact on the economy, businesses, and people's lives. When Lawmakers do not put enough consideration or research into drafting public policy, those policies can have a significant negative impact on the income, employment, and futures of private citizens, in addition to funding for State services. A later chapter on social responsibility looks at a number of instances in which law makers do not fully understand the consequences of their decisions or the damage their policies are doing to communities and local economies.

1

The Meaning of Responsibility

Responsibility is more than an attribution, like credit or blame, for a decision. In an earlier chapter on critical thinking skills, we looked at how the ability to make a good decision depends on whether you have enough knowledge to predict whether a decision will result in a positive or negative outcome. But to make a responsible decision, you have to not only understand the consequences of that decision, you have to be willing to accept responsibility for those consequences. When you are given a responsibility, you are given ownership of performing a task in addition to responsibility for all related decisions and consequences, so that you can be held accountable for those consequences.

Sometimes, as a result of social influences or poor habits, people are lazy and do not take enough responsibility for their role in causing the outcomes in their lives. Or they make decisions based on beliefs that lead to mistakes and incorrect conclusions about the consequences of a decision. Many reasons exist for why a person may be unable to predict or understand the consequences of decision. To start with, people have natural cognitive limitations or cognitive impairments that may prevent them from seeing the full consequences of their decisions. Some examples of cognitive limitations that prevent people from operating responsibly, include early child development, age-related conditions like Alzheimer's disease, mental disabilities, or mental disorders.

Irresponsible behavior is usually indicative of not caring about, or refusing to accept responsibility for, the consequences of one's decisions. A common example of this is when a person does not know, or care, how one's decisions negatively impact people's lives. This is more common among criminals, who victimize and hurt people for their own gain. But, sadly, business managers, politicians, and leaders can be equally immoral and unethical. For instance, when a business manager attempts to save money by not caring how contaminated food could make people sick. Decisionmakers may be, particularly, careless about how decisions impact people which they have a low opinion, negative biases, and negative attitudes.

## 2
## Attributing Responsibility

Attributing responsibility is a process of identifying the root cause of a problem or situation. This is similar to how police detectives identify who, or what, is responsible for a crime. But when you look at your own life problems, you have to consider whether those problems were caused by our own choices, or by forces beyond your control. Being able to diagnose the root cause of the problem correctly, can enable you to more effectively resolve those problems.

People are not always able to diagnose the causes of problems, and attribute responsibility correctly. For instance, a tennis player who is frustrated and playing a terrible game suddenly blames it on the tennis racket. Or Tim who is late to work and is cut off by a slow driver, gets angry at the driver who really did nothing wrong. Tim is really the one responsible for planning his morning drive and arriving at work on time. And people face more complex problems in which they do not understand how their own decisions create the problems in their lives.

Other times, people see themselves as being responsible for things they have no control over. For example, a mother feeling guilty for her child's sickness from an unknown illness and wonders what she did wrong to deserve it. Or a crime victim may say that he did not protect himself enough from the criminal who harmed him. He is not responsible for committing the crime and should not take responsibility for the consequences, even when he could have done more to protect himself.

A person's scope of responsibility encompasses what that person has control over and is able to be responsible for. Your scope of responsibility is not entirely static in that it can be extended by taking more control, and more responsibility, for more things in your life. For example, you could take more control of your development by developing a new skillset. And that could give you greater control and certainty over the direction of your life, and your ability to earn an income, rather than relying on luck and wishful thinking.

But people can also very helpless and powerless over the forces of nature. All people live with some sense of power-lessness and an ever-present sense that life is shaped by forces beyond their control. Not only are you unable to control the forces of nature, you do not have control over your own biology and cognitive limitations, making it impossible to foresee the consequences of every decision. But you do have control over your own choices. And the next couple of sections expand on this idea by looking at you as a product of circumstances, and you as a product of your own making.

## 3
## A Product of Circumstance

You are not responsible for everything that happens to you as your life is shaped by fortunate opportunities and unfortunate events that influence the course of your life in uncontrollable ways. You do not have a choice about your genes, or the political or economic conditions you were born into. You do not have control over the environment in which you grew up. And you cannot control past events, what people think, or the help you receive.

Throughout your life, you will be forced to relinquish control and responsibility to other people. For example, caregivers make choices for children that influenced the course of the child's life. Or, in your job, you may be under the direction of a manager. If you have a doctor, you may be following the advice of the doctor.

People also tend to develop in response to their environment. My experience living in difference cities has taught me that people who live in poorer, higher crime-rate, communities tend to be more protective, defensive, and less trusting toward strangers, than people who live in wealthier, lower crime-rate, communities. Different conditions present different challenges, elicit different responses, provide different opportunities, promote different personality traits, and lead to different life-altering decisions.

4
A Product of Choice

In addition to being a product of circumstance, you are also a product of your choices. Many of those choices include your development, your productivity, skills, and helping other people. You have a choice in how you serve other people in your life roles, as a citizen, employee, manager, parent, or leader. And you may not have a choice about the problems you face, but you have some choice in how you resolve those problems.

People's choices determine their successes and failures. When watching a sports match, a sports reporter may focus on the player's decisions in the last seconds of the game that caused the team to win or lose. But many factors actually contributed to the team's victory or defeat, like practice, diet, exercise, and strategy. Games are sometimes won or lost before the players step onto the field. And improving performance with physical conditioning, testing abilities, reducing uncertainty, and having determination and persistence, all influences the final result.

In a marketing environment, like here in the United States, consumers are continuously bombarded by advertisements enticing them to consume unhealthy food and beverages. Since those advertisements do not force people to do anything those ads cannot be entirely blamed for people's unhealthy diet or poor choices. You will find plenty examples of people who live in that same marketing environment who make healthy lifestyle choices. But what can profoundly influence people's choices is their education and knowhow. When people know how to live healthier, they are more likely to make healthier lifestyle choices.

5

Answering for Decisions

The desire for social acceptance, and the desire to avoid rejection, influences how people answer for, and accept responsibility for, their decisions. In any human society, you will find people striving for social approval, striving to be polite when interacting with people, taking care of their positions, and striving to be successful in their occupation. And this striving can be exhausting if you are in a constant battle to keep up with a demanding schedule, or are constantly responding to the demands of family members or your employer. It always seems like you could do a little more, work a little harder, or be a little more prepared, in the process of succeeding or failing in your lifegoals. So, inevitably, you make mistakes and have shortcomings. But how you answer for those mistakes or shortcomings demonstrates how responsible you are as a person, and how well you perform your life roles.

One way of answering for mistakes and shortcomings is by being honest and accepting full responsibility. A person who wants to perform at a high level may want objective feedback about mistakes and shortcomings, so those problems can be resolved and improvements can be made. This mindset ensures that if mistakes are made, that those mistakes do not carry over into the future.

Unfortunately, not everybody thinks this way. Rather

than putting in the work to resolve mistakes and shortcomings, a person may see the negative consequences of a decision as an attack on one's character, and potentially a loss of employment. So, the person may lie, or deny responsibility, for poor decisions. That is especially true if a law was broken, or a decision caused significant and irreparable loss. Defendants in criminal trials often try to lie to deny responsibility for a crime to avoid punishment. The problem with denying responsibility, especially in a professional workplace, is that it leaves problems unresolved.

## 6
## Character Defenses

A *character defense*, or *defense mechanism*, is an attempt to protect one's interests and influence outcomes, by defending one's decisions from accusations of negligence or wrongdoing. In an earlier chapter on motivation, we looked at the effect of gains and losses on a person's emotions, relationships, and overall behavior. People get very angry and dramatic when defending their actions and protecting their interests from condemning accusations to avoid rejection and adverse treatment, in addition to personal, employment, and financial losses.

On an instinctive level, the display of anger is an emotional defense, the outward characteristics of which provides physical and emotional protection. Physiologist Walter Cannon once described the defense of anger as expressing itself in the bristling of hair and uncovering of teeth in rage and hostility. The "rage response," as he called it, is displayed in a "crouching body," a "frowning brow," and "grinding teeth." The individual mutters "growled threats," has "tightened fists," and seizes a weapon in preparation for attack. All of these behaviors, he says, are useful in preparation for the struggle.[9]

People are usually not that overly dramatic when they get angry. But fear, and the desire for protection, compels people to thoughtlessly pulverize any pestilent little thing that threatens their interests, no matter how small or insignificant it is. This desire for protection is territorial, in a way, because people try to protect things that could be taken from them, like employment, an intimate relationship, or a material possession, which provokes a response to defend it, or take it back. A child may express this tendency most uninhibitedly when a toy or food is taken away, especially when the child begins to cry, kick, or scream, because someone threatens to deprive him of the thing he wants. Adults behave similarly when they throw fits, lie, or start arguments, to get what they want.

Your natural defenses are continuously working to protect you from physical, social, and financial threats. And people are naturally compelled to defend their decisions, especially when those decisions are believed to be based on sound reasoning. When a person makes a terrible decision that results in horrendous or devastating consequences, that person may not want to accept responsibility for the consequences because of the negative attribution it could ascribe to one's character, which could threaten one's freedom, trustworthiness, or livelihood. So, the easiest way to avoid accepting responsibility for an unfair loss is to either show how the act was not deliberate, or by denying that one committed the act in the first place. These defenses are sometimes used in criminal trials where the defendant claims self-defense for a violent act, or completely denies committing the act. The following sections look at a few character defenses that people use to either accept, or avoid accepting, responsibility for their decisions, and how people use deception to protect their interests.

7

Rationalization

Rationalization is a character defense that attempts to prove that one's actions were based on valid and justifiable reasons to prevent adverse judgment and treatment. Eric Fromm gave an example of how the "function of rationalization," as he called it, enables a person to "prove to himself and to others that his action is determined by reason, common sense, or at least conventional morality." And no matter how "unreasonable or immoral an action may be, man has an insuperable urge to rationalize it."[25] History provides many examples of people who perceived themselves as righteous and justified in everything they did, no matter how wrongful, hurtful, or destructive they were.

Alfred Adler gave another example of a person who wanted to deny ever making mistakes and, instead, wanted to blame his parents or education. He complained that nobody ever cared for him and that he was mistreated. He wanted to be "excused of further responsibility" to avoid all criticism and blame. The reason he could never fulfill his life ambitions was always someone else's fault. He never changed his behavior, but "turns and twists and distorts his experiences until they fit it." Even the child, Adler said, creates excuses for his failures, claiming that he was "too weak or petted," or siblings thwarted his development.[1]

The fact that our personal development is, to some extent, shaped and nurtured by other people, like caregivers, educators, trainers, and managers, makes it easy to pass blame onto them for our shortcomings. And despite the fact that, as an adult, you are responsible for your own personal development, some people take rationalization to its furthest extent and blame all of their problems on anything that is larger or more powerful than themselves.

In the book *Totem and Taboo*, Sigmund Freud called this tendency a "delusion of persecution," in which a person's power over life-circumstances is so immensely exaggerated that every disagreeable experience falls under the responsibility of the more powerful person. He pointed out that savages blamed their kings because they had enormous power and, therefore, power over the forces of nature. This, he said, arose from the heavy burden of being dependent on someone who is more powerful, where it puts the individual in a position of blame for all misfortunes.[24]

Blame can also go in the other direction, when the leader blames subordinates for problems that arise under one's leadership. Managers are responsible for making sure their workers are sufficiently trained. But managers could also blame workers, technological complexity, or circumstances beyond their control, when the organization consistently fails or performs poorly as a result of the leader's incompetence. A manager may blame the labor market, or labor shortages, for not supplying enough talented labor. When a manager is truly qualified and a skilled professional, the manager should have no problem taking responsibility for the quality of the work performed, and ensuring the organization is performing at a high level.

8

Manipulation

Manipulation is a character defense that exploits weakness in human judgment by attempting to alter perceptions (i.e., by saying anything necessary) to influence an outcome. People learn how to manipulate people and their perceptions at an early age, when children throw screaming fits to get what they want, or learn to act differently around people who provide attention or money.

Manipulation is not always used for malicious reasons. Marketing and political campaigns often try to influence the choices of buyers or voters by altering their perceptions. A sign in front of a restaurant may say that it is the #1 Hot Dog Restaurant in Town for 30 years, despite the fact that it is consistently rated as the worst restaurant in town. Businesses exaggerate the greatness of their products to attract customers. Similarly, elected officials exaggerate their accomplishments to win voters. History tells a long story of people manipulating their way into power, and saying anything to manipulate people's perceptions to get what they want.

In the words of Niccolo Machiavelli in his book *the Prince*, "men judge by the eye rather than the hand, for all men can see a thing, but few come close enough to touch it. All men will see what you seem to be; only a few will know what you are, and those few will not dare to oppose the many who have the majesty of the state on their side to defend them. In all men's acts"..."it is the result that renders the verdict when there is no court of appeal."[38]

In the criminal world, the con-artist exploits this weakness in judgment for the purpose committing crimes, like illicitly obtaining money or property. The con-artist lies by assuming a false identity to gain unauthorized access to information or possessions, or manipulates perceptions to avoid being caught. Or an abuser may frame a victim as someone who is crazy, genetically defective, mentally unstable, mentally deficient, or as someone who cannot be believed or trusted.

## 9

## Obstruction

Obstruction is a character defense that tries to cover-over and hide undesirable behaviors or character flaws that could subject a person to accusations of wrongfulness or guilt. This would be similar to a murderer hiding a murder weapon in a crime novel. Using obstruction, people attempt to influence outcomes by preventing others from seeing the truth, or hiding anything that would be incriminating or would attribute wrongdoing.

Obstruction can also be learned during childhood. The child wants to please the caregiver who provides food, playthings, and safety. And when something is accidentally broken, the child learns to hide it and act innocent to prevent the caregiver's anger and displeasure. Even as a child grows into adulthood, young people learn that they can get ahead by hiding weaknesses, insecurities, and guilt, and using deception to avoid admitting shortcomings. People want to accept responsibility for the positive things they do, not the terrible things that subject them to condemning judgment or punishment.

Obstruction often hides behavioral patterns that are socially unacceptable, like substance abuse or domestic violence. Those patterns may emerge in the presence of different people in different environments. A person, who is a monster to a family member, may be the kindest and most caring person to managers and coworkers, depending on the nature of the relationship, and what they stand to gain or lose from the relationship.

Repression is a method of obstructing oneself from one's own problems. And sometimes, repression can be beneficial, like when a person feels guilt and regret for their failures, mistakes, inadequacies, or inappropriate desires. Repression allows them to overcome unnecessary guilt and move on with life. But repression can also do unnecessary harm and work against the welfare of people. For example, if a person ignores physical pain that turns out to be a cancerous tumor. Or, if a person ignores a loud bang that turns out to be a murder.

10

Taking Responsibility

Taking responsibility means increasing your scope of responsibility by attempting to take more control over the things in your life. Doing so can allow you to have more control over your fate, rather than allowing other people or circumstances to control your fate. Ideally, you want to have some choice about the direction of your life. And you can certainly have choice about the development of your abilities, skills, and overall performance. By working harder to improve those skills, you stand a better chance at making things happen, rather than allowing things to happen to you and being dissatisfied with the end result.

Parents sometimes encourage their children to take more responsibility by showing how their actions have consequences, by requiring them to do household chores. Some of those may include cleaning, staying organized, and how they treat other people. But it also involves avoiding excuses from responsibility, or blaming forces beyond your control.

Taking more control over your life involves making

things happen, rather than waiting for things to happen. If you wait for that lucky moment when fortune changes your life, then you will always have bad luck, and unfortunate circumstances, to blame for your lack of success. You also have to develop the knowhow, and the required skillset, to make things happen. A business manager, for example, could blame a decline in sales and revenue on market demand, instead of making the product more appealing, or diversifying their investments. Or a manager may blame a shortage of talent on the labor market when they could be developing talent internally.

Taking more control over your life starts with understanding how your choices contributed to your current situation, rather than focusing on how misfortune and forces beyond your control created your current situation. If you are unable to recognize your role in causing a failure, which may be attributed to your lack of effort or knowhow, then you will never be motivated to change the way you operate to prevent those failures from occurring in the future.

To illustrate this idea, imagine you purchase take-out food from a local restaurant. You get home and notice an item is wrong and a family member is upset and will not eat the food. At first, you blame the worker who put the order together. But you also had responsibility to make sure the order was correct before leaving. You could have discovered and corrected the mistake and left with the order you paid for. You will not be satisfied with your life if you allow other people to make too many decisions for you. And those people will always be to blame for the problems you experience as a result.

Where possible, you should try to seek objective feedback about problems or shortcomings in your performance. A great example of this is students who receive grades in school. Grades reveal areas of development that students need to improve so they can invest more time developing those knowledge gaps. If a student performs poorly and blames it on the instructor, accusing the instructor of being too difficult, or for not helping the students prepare more, then the student will never take enough responsibility for one's own performance to improve in the future. Not receiving this type of feedback means that one's performance is a matter of opinion, which is heavily influenced by biases and character defenses.

And lastly, identify and resolve problems in your life that lead to dissatisfaction. If you are unhappy with your living conditions, think of how you could change your living conditions to make you happier. If you are unhappy with money or transportation, think of solutions to those problems and put those solutions in place. Striving to overcome the causes of dissatisfaction reduces the number of things you have to blame for the dissatisfaction you experience in life.

## 11
## Giving Responsibility

Delegating responsibility involves letting another person, or business, take responsibility for completing a task. You cannot know everything. And you can be more effective, and more productive, if you delegate tasks to other people, who are able to perform that task better than you can. But that also means trusting people, having confidence in their abilities, and giving responsibility.

The ability to work as a team means getting more done in less time. People who live in developed economies do not make all of their meals or possessions. Instead, they delegate responsibility to people who specialize in those tasks. A single person could do the work of ten people, but it would take ten times as long, if not longer. Delegating tasks to other people allows you to accomplish more in less time at a higher quality of production, which allows you to pursue more goals.

If you are delegating responsibility for a task that you perform, provide training on how to effectively perform that role and be responsive if that person has questions. The fact that you may have figured out how to perform that role yourself is great. But expecting someone else to do the same does not ensure that task is performed well, and it does not ensure the quality of production.

Delegate responsibility for tasks beyond your skillset. If you have an appliance break, you may be able to fix it yourself. But, unless you are an expert, your knowledge of appliance repair is not going to be as good as an expert who repairs appliances for a living. Instead of spending hours trying to fix it, and not knowing if you have the tools, you would be better off delegating that task to a professional appliance repair person.

When delegating responsibility, establish some type of obligation (i.e., a social expectation, a verbal agreement, or a formal contract) with the person responsible for carrying out the task. Establishing some type of formal agreement with the people you are delegating responsibilities to forms an agreement about the work to be performed. And that enables the person performing the work to know the deliverables to be expected. And it creates a reasonable basis for termination if the agreement is broken.

12

Accountability

Accountability is the ability to attribute personal responsibility to an outcome. Just as an Accountant keeps a system of ledgers to record business decisions that involve revenues and expenditures, people are able to keep a mental ledger of their own contributions and those of other people.

The criminal justice system, for example, is a system of accountability that punishes people for causing harm to people or the community. The legal system provides services to victims of crimes to prevent perpetrators from repeating crimes, or to help victims recover from unfair losses. The news media can also be instrumental in holding people accountable for their actions. Without that accountability for decisions, like dumping toxic chemicals in a river, people would have no way of knowing about the existence of those activities, and nothing would be done about it.

A system of accountability, or merit system, can be an effective management tool for measuring financial gains and losses and personal contributions, but only if management values and promotes people based on merit, skills, and expertise. This means giving credit where credit is due, and identifying people who make decisions that benefit, and add value to, the organization. And it also means policing actions that cause harm, conflict, negligence, and preventable losses to the businesses or its reputation. This also ensures managers are experienced, knowledgeable, and know what they are doing, workers are better trained, and teams are capable of producing quality goods or services that meet the needs of management and the organization.

Incentive systems that reward (or compensate) contributions that add value to the business, or takes corrective action for decisions that negatively impact the business, can be instrumental in driving organizational performance. Studies have shown that rewarding workers for positive contributions, acknowledges the value of their work, and leads to improved employee satisfaction and better retention. Providing rewards when workers deserve it validates their contributions and encourages employees to repeat those behaviors.[57]

## 13
### Failures of Accountability

A failure of accountability occurs when an abuse of privilege, an abuse of power, or an ethics violation, goes unaccounted for. Abuses, or ethics violations, usually cause someone to experience an unfair loss, like a loss of physical security, illicitly taking money from the business, committing fraud, assault, and other ethics violations.

Every organization has unique set of problems created by the unique individuals and beliefs of those who manage the organization. Many of those problems stem from management practices, like being indifferent about whether abuses are happening so long as operations continue to function. People are, sometimes, dishonest because they do not want to put in the effort to advancing their skills, but still want advancement within the organization. They may even use various tactics to increase their job security, like hiring lesser skilled candidates.

Failures of accountability often occur when officials, who have the power and authority to write rules, systematically exempt themselves, or other people, from having to answer for their decisions. Systematic exemption from accountability is found in organizations where favoritism (e.g., unfair discrimination) is allowed because of cronyism, family relation, ethnic background, gender, or race. A manager may hire a friend, or return a favor to a friend by hiring a relative, to a management position. This creates an environment where management favors and unconditionally trusts certain individuals who are free to abuse their position, harm workers, or harm the business, without any oversight or accountability.

Many types of problems occur as a result of a lack of accountability. When ethics violations are allowed to occur with no consequences, it emboldens unethical behavior and becomes part of the organizational culture, especially when those abusive behaviors are seen as acceptable and normal. And that has a negative impact on the workforce as a result of malicious treatment, and unfair losses, which may cause a decline in worker satisfaction, a decline in productivity, a decline in cooperation and communication, increased conflict and fighting, and a lower employee retention rate.

Organizations will allow for failures of accountability for a number of reasons. Some management philosophies promote empowerment and trusting managers to run their team as if they were running their own company. And that can result in a lack of management oversight and management neglect, which allows for mismanagement, abuses of privileges, and violating company policies, without accountability.

When organizations allow for failures of accountability, it becomes impossible to hold people accountable for abuses and ethics violations, even when they cause significant harm or losses. Even when laws exist to prevent violators from committing ethics violations, it can be difficult to prove unless every personal interaction is recorded with a device. And that makes it difficult, if not impossible, to show an ongoing pattern of abuse. When violations are impossible to prove, management and human resources people find that ignoring the violation, or firing the accuser, is far easier to make the problem go away, than taking it seriously.

Another problem with reporting workplace abuses is that people have belief biases, and are inclined to disbelieve an accusation that does not match their cognitive model of how reality works. Consider the company Theranos, which attracted billions of dollars of investment, achieving a $10 billion valuation during a 10-year-period. The business was able to attract funding by convincing people that they had developed a new blood analysis technology that did not work as promised. Using these dishonest tactics to attract wealthy investors, the company was able to hire talented professionals and even employ high-ranking government officials, all while the founder was regularly featured in magazines and on television for her success.

The reason investors had so much confidence in Theranos had to do with a belief bias, and the belief that a business would not gain so much attention and investment if it did not have a sound business model. That belief, of course, turned out to be wrong. And if a highly-public and openly scrutinized business, like Theranos, could get away with it, then what do you think happens in small-to-medium sized businesses that are not under such public scrutiny? Do you think that management in those businesses are all saintly people who make rational and sound decisions? Not all of them. But people certainly want to believe they do. And rather than putting in the effort to investigate accusations, sadly, management and human resources may simply disbelieve accusations of wrongdoing.

Failures of accountability also happen when States pass laws, like At-Will employment laws, that give people or organizations the power to abuse their privileges without consequences. They, essentially, give managers the freedom to hire, deny employment, or fire an employee without just cause. Under At-Will employment laws, managers working under the protected name of the employer are assumed to be operating fairly, honestly, and with care, while being allowed to freely abuse and dispose of workers without care, and no accountability or consequences.

This lack of employee protections creates a type of lawlessness that defeats the purpose of a criminal justice system, which is supposed to protect people from unfair losses. Managers are free to cause substantial damage a person's career, income, and professional reputation, by terminating the person's employment and lying about the reasons for dismissal. Even when employee protection laws exist, lawyers may not pursue those cases because they are difficult to win. So, employees have no way of showing abusive employers that what they are doing is wrong, and no way of preventing the employer from doing it again.

# CHAPTER VII:
# PERSONAL SKILLS

Personal relationships consist of people who cooperate in pursuit of a shared or common interest. Achieving certain life goals, like earning an income, having a family, or running a successful business, requires the cooperation of people who make those things possible. Personal relationships provide psychological and practical benefits, like needed help, emotional support, positive experiences, and the perception that everything will be alright. And they can give your life greater meaning and purpose as you are needed by your friends, family, or coworkers.

But while some behaviors improve cooperation, others interfere with cooperation. And personal skills tend to be those that improve cooperation. So, this chapter explores how personal skills, like social skills, communication skills, or conflict resolution skills, improve cooperation and enable people to build healthy relationships.

1
Healthy Relationships

A healthy relationship is one that makes everyone better-off as a result of being in the relationship. One way of doing that is by respecting the wishes of those involved, even when those wishes differ from your own. You also need to protect yourself from harm, and from people who would make you worse-off, by establishing rules for what you are willing to accept. For example, not tolerating, or cooperating with, someone who would steal from you, or who would physically harm you.

Much of childhood development is a process of learning these socially acceptable rules for getting what you want. Adults commonly want food, sex, and protection. But most people do not obtain those things by maliciously attacking people or committing crimes. That would only make the victims of those acts worse-off, and may motivate them to retaliate, to prevent the perpetrator from doing it again. So, learning how to develop healthy relationships, and learning how to make everyone better-off as a result of being in the relationship, is a set of skills that can be developed and improved.

## 2
## Social Skills

Social skills and communication skills are the means by which people cooperate. The lack of effective communication skills causes an inability to cooperate toward shared goals and causes misunderstandings. In business, it causes organizational dysfunction, business failures, and the management's inability to identify and resolve problems. And those problems can cause a decline in productivity, a loss of worker satisfaction, client satisfaction, and revenue.

Communication skills are developed just like any other skill, by testing your ability with practice and receiving feedback. Feedback is necessary to improve communication because it enables you to gain insight into areas where you need improvement that you would, otherwise, overlook. And that feedback can come in the form of body language, in emotional and verbal responses. Listening, itself, is a communication skill that allows people to receive feedback, share ideas, expertise, and to see things from other perspectives.

How a message is delivered and interpreted often determines how well that message is received. If Sandra disagrees with a new departmental policy and expresses that disagreement by verbally attacking the idea, the audience may take a defensive stance and stop being receptive to the attack. But if she presents the problem as an opportunity for improvement, and shows how everyone benefits from changing the policy, the audience may have more interest in listening.

3

Emotional Skills

Emotional skills, sometimes call emotional intelligence, is the ability to effectively convey and recognize emotions. The way you make people feel, and the emotions you evoke, is a skill that can be developed with practice. And developing those skills requires self-awareness of how you make other people feel and how they interpret your behavior.

People with highly developed emotional skills are able to separate feelings about their own life from how they treat other people. If you are upset about a problem or are having a rough day, it should not influence how you treat other people. If it does, then your behavior may be interpreted as threatening, or upset with them, which would convey the wrong message.

155

In business, the way management treats workers can influence job satisfaction and productivity. Some evidence suggests that when workers have low expectations and low confidence in their abilities, those feelings decrease motivation and productivity. Psychologists call this the Galatea effect, or the self-fulfilling prophecy. In other words, when a person has low self-confidence, and has a fear of failure, that person is more likely to fail.

On the other hand, when management expresses high expectations and high confidence in their worker's abilities, self-confidence and productivity can increase. Psychologists call this the Pygmalion effect, or the power of expectations. When workers are treated like they are capable of succeeding, they are more likely to succeed. When management treats workers like they cannot succeed, that discouragement may prevent them from trying. Or, even worse, when workers are harshly threated, their sense of obligation to the organization may deteriorate, which could negatively influence their attitudes and productivity.

4

Trust & Confidence

Trust is the ability to rely on someone to act in your interests, rather of acting against your interests. According to a 2012 study by internet search engine company Google, trust influences workplace productivity more than any other factor. Their study, which they called Project Aristotle, primarily focused on what made the most productive and creative teams. And despite different personality types, what made for the most productive teams were those that created a "safe environment" in which members were allowed to take risks, propose new ideas, and make suggestions in meetings, without being subjected to feelings of negative judgment or harmful criticism.[17]

Teamwork requires trust, and the ability to depend on team members without suspecting that those involved may be working against their interests. When people feel like they, or their ideas, are being attacked, the instinct is to fight or flee, which tends to erode cooperation among team members. Maintaining a beneficial relationship in which everyone is made better-off, requires respecting other people's interests and viewpoints, and allowing them to contribute to the team.

Having confidence in a person's abilities can also improve cooperation. That confidence may be built when people follow through on their promises, when they deliver as expected, and when they demonstrate the skills to perform a role.

## 5
## Conflict Resolution Skills

Conflict occurs as a result of taking an opposing side in a dispute. And conflict is part of the human condition as people are motivated to protect and defend their interests from threats by avoiding sources of danger or counter-attacking. People create conflicts over just about anything you can imagine, whether it is territorial control, political disagreements, the use of funds, or ideas. A married couple, for example, may argue or disagree about how their time and money should be spent. And that disagreement can escalate into a conflict.

Out of all the other factors that deteriorate cooperation

in relationships, including a loss of trust or confidence, conflict can be the most harmful when it results in some form of personal attack. An attack could be a verbal or legal attack, or could escalate in to physical violence. Attacks motivate people to seek revenge and counter-attack. And when those conflicts continue to escalate overtime, they can become increasingly more hostile and damaging, which makes them very destructive. So, the ability to resolve conflict can prevent further negative and unnecessary consequences.

Conflict resolution requires resolving the root causes of opposition. One cleaver way of doing that is to get on your opponent's side, empathize, and ask questions that may enable you to view the situation from the other person's perspective. Getting on the side of your opponent may seem counterintuitive. But conflicts rapidly evaporate when a person sees that you are not against them. People do not listen to their opponents or enemies. They listen to their allies. So, you are never going to effectively influence a person by siding against that person.

During my younger years in customer service, this approach worked very effectively for me. Rather than mindlessly arguing with a customer, as many of my coworkers did, my approach involved getting on the customer's side by agreeing with the customer, and seeing things from the customer's perspective. This did not mean that I simply did anything the customer wanted and gave into the customer's every wish. But instead it meant representing the customer as best I could within the organization in accordance with company policy. Even when a customer would call in angry and screaming, when the person saw that I was not fighting them on the issue, the person would very quickly settle down, apologize, and begin to listen. Coworkers always suspected me of cheating because of my high call-resolution rate.

To avoid inflaming tensions, you also need to get over your emotions and focus on producing the desired outcome, rather than winning the conflict. Most things are not worth arguing over. And winning an argument is not the same as creating the best outcome for everyone. Rather than perpetuating senseless conflict, focus on the goal you are trying to achieve and the outcome you are trying to create.

If all else fails, find an intermediary, like a therapist, counselor, or attorney, which can be an expensive but an effective approach. Intermediaries can be instrumental when you want to maintain a relationship, like a marriage or business relationship, but have irresoluble conflicts. The intermediary can look at the problem from an unemotional and objective perspective, to create a compromise that makes everyone better-off.

# 6
# Unhealthy Relationships

Unhealthy relationships make people worse-off as a result of being in the relationship, and usually as a result of being harmed, victimized, or abused in some way. People usually do not intend to get involved with harmful relationships. Once the relationship is established and those involved depend on each other as a team, it becomes difficult to end that relationship. And that becomes a problem when one person is psychologically or physically harmed by the other person.

When mistreatment is frequent enough, it can cause mental disorders. Memories of that mistreatment can cause a person to harbor negative feelings. When a person begins to predict attacks, it can cause that person to behave defensively, avoid the person, or launch counter-attacks. And when a person feels trapped in the relationship, it can cause depression, a sense of helplessness, despair, and emotional problems.

In some circumstances, ending an unhealthy relationship can be difficult, if not impossible. Married couples who have children stand to lose a substantial amount of financial support, a standard of living, their child's education, and a retirement. Finding a new partner may become difficult. Or one partner may threaten retaliation or physical violence, if the other partner ends the relationship. And for these reasons, people stay in unhealthy relationships until the conflict is so intense that it becomes mentally and physically damaging.

Early in the relationship, if you are able to form an agreement about the pursuit of shared interests, and the conditions upon which the relationship will be terminated, it can shape expectations and reduce the element of surprise. If you are in an unhealthy relationship, you need find a way to make it healthy, or find a way out, before it negatively affects your mental or physical health. And that may require the help of intermediaries, like a professional counselor or friends.

# CHAPTER VIII:
# STRESS MANAGEMENT

*Stress management skills*, or *coping skills*, are techniques for controlling or avoiding negative forms of stress. Some forms of stress can be healthy stress that reinforces your condition, and some of it can do harm. But how you manage stress, how you handle negativity, difficulties, and frustrations, has an influence on your productivity, relationships, and how you perform your roles. How do you respond if people treat you unfairly, or are abusing their privileges? Do you respond by flying-off-the-handle in a fit of rage? Do you ruminate about those instances and harbor resentment? Or do you binge drink?

The inability to manage stress and emotions can impair judgment and cause poor and impulsive decisions. A lack of coping skills can result in angry outbursts, relationship problems, reckless driving, and fatal accidents. A person who lacks coping skills may see a decline in productivity, or may suddenly end relationships or employment. All of these can cause substantial losses in terms of opportunities, personal relationships, and income. And more importantly, they can cause a decline in self-confidence, a poorer outlook on life, and an overall decline in personal health and development. According to the American Institute of Stress, distress causes crime, violence, unhealthy behaviors, and loneliness, and is responsible for the majority of visits to primary care physicians.[4] So, identifying and managing negative forms of stress can dramatically improve your wellbeing and longevity.

And the first sections of this chapter look at different types of stress and the impact that stress has on people's lives. The last sections of this chapter look at some stress management techniques.

1
Stressors

*Stressors* are experiences, events, or memories that place greater demand on your mental and physical abilities. Stressors could be daily difficulties, or dangers that evoke fear and anxiety, shortages of time and money, a lack of cooperation, conflicts, and unfair losses. Stressors can have physical effects as a result of muscle tension, or psychological effects, like emotional stressors.

How you perceive sources of distress, and how frequently you experience it, can change your reaction. Do you see a problem as an insurmountable problem? Or do you see the same problem relatively doable, and a matter of effort and perseverance? Do you overreact and become emotional? Or do you stay calm and collected and form a strategy for solving the problem?

A person who lacks coping skills, and lacks different ways of looking at the same problems, can create more negative consequences that continues to escalate distress. For example, a person who is late to work, may drive aggressively and cause an accident, or receive a traffic ticket. Or, when faced with dozens of work-related demands, that person may panic and retreat, or attack coworkers. Negative stress reactions can evoke stress in other people as well, especially if a person resorts to blaming, hurling accusations of wrongdoing, or creating unrealistic demands.

## 2
## Positive & Negative Stressors

Whether a stressor is positive or negative depends on whether it leads to a positive or negative change in your condition. Stress is not always harmful. Positive stressors, for example, are those that lead to positive change, physically or emotionally. They tend to promote personal growth and development, improve decision-making, and result in wanted outcomes. Taking on difficulties, challenging yourself, and learning, are all positive forms of stress required for your normal growth and development. Eustress, which is aroused by stimulating and thrilling activities, like sports or entertainment, is a form of stress that is physically and emotionally beneficial. Emotional stressors, like anger, which can be negative stressors, can also be beneficial when it motivates you to make change in your life, or make a difference in the community. Other forms of positive stress may include wakefulness, excitement, and exerting effort, which can release hormones, like DHEA, which is believed to stimulate brain growth and brain development.

Negative stressors are those that harm growth and development and impair judgement, cause poor decisions, cause problems in personal relationships, cause a decline in productivity and income, and result in unwanted losses. A significant part of coping with negative stress is how you handle negative circumstances, threats to your interests, things that frustrate you to anger, significant losses, and decisions that have a negative impact on your life. That can be especially difficult when those actions are particularly hurtful and damaging. Every day, you are likely to experience offensive behaviors, like road-rage, verbal abuse, crimes against you, or conflicting viewpoints. Or you will find people who are behaving defensively and denying wrongdoing, refusing to accept responsibility for creating a problem, or lying to make-up for shortcomings in performing a job. And the way you confront or avoid those problems can determine whether you make yourself better, or worse, off.

Significant emotional stressors can cause emotional disturbances that are characteristic of mental disorders. Extreme emotions can lead to impulsive fight-or-flight decisions that do not consider the longer-term consequences. Extreme anger, for example, can cause a person to suddenly quit a job, violently attack another person, or behave recklessly and irresponsibly.

3
Chronic Stress

Chronic stress is distress that is experienced frequently as a result of work-related demands, personal treatment, the constant threat of crime, mental disorders, and other causes of frequent distress. Chronic stress also causes emotional and behavioral problems, including finger biting, emotional instability, altered eating and sleeping patterns, the use of alcohol or other drugs, and law enforcement intervention.[11]

When negative forms of distress are experienced frequently enough, they actually do damage to a person's brain and body. Fears and worries, for example, tend increase heart rate and breathing, and mobilize the body for action, all of which places greater demand on the body's internal systems to work harder and move faster. During a stressful event, the nervous system discharges hormones from the endocrine glands, including the hypothalamus, adrenal, and pituitary glands, which are responsible for survival instincts, like emotions, alertness, excitement, aggression, and metabolism. After a distressing episode, the body activates the parasympathetic nervous system to restore homeostasis and stabilize bodily functions and return the body back to its normal stress levels.

When these stress reactions are repeated frequently enough to be considered chronic, they can be linked to psychosomatic disorders, which are physical illnesses caused by alterations in biological function, body chemistry, immune suppression disease, and other diseases. Stress causes muscle tension, increases heart rate and blood pressure, blood sugar rises, blood is directed away from the gut where it is normally needed for digestion, and it clots more easily. The American Institute of Stress says that chronic stress may lead to hypertension, heart attacks, strokes, diabetes, and other problems.[5]

4
Fear & Stress

Fear is one of the more powerful and compelling influences on behavior. Fear is evoked by the perception of a threat to personal interests, like the loss of physical safety, the loss of time or money, or missed deadlines. If you want to finish a project on time and within budget, and the time constraints begin to work against your interests, it may evoke fear and distress, and may spur you to work faster, concentrate harder, and work longer hours to complete the project. People also experience stress as they strive to achieve goals, keep appointments, satisfy the demands of employers and clients, and create the outcomes they want.

When faced with a threat, you have a few choices: You could combat the threat, escape the threat, or play dead. This is known as the fight-or-flight response, which influences how you engage or avoid the challenges presented by circumstances. In its most extreme and exaggerated forms, the fight-or-flight response can manifest in murder, to annihilate a perceive threat, or suicide in flight from the stresses, burdens, and hardships of living. But usually, fight-or-flight responses are revealed in smaller, less noticeable, forms like when a person develops a habit of conflict or avoidance toward certain people or situations.

Fear can work for you, or work against you, depending on how you respond to those threats. Fear works for you when it keeps you safe, helps you assess when situations are too risky, and compels you to behave responsibly. Fear about potential future outcomes (i.e., destitution, poverty, or loneliness), compels people to be productive, develop skills, seek employment, and develop beneficial relationships. So, in many ways, fear about future outcomes can motivate you to be more responsible and dependable, and can enable you to make decisions that prevent loss and hardship.

But fear also works against you, especially if you habitually respond to difficulties or urgency with extreme emotion rather than deliberate reason. Excessive fear can make people flighty or combative, which can impair thinking, judgment, and rational decision-making. Fear can cause a person to overreact in overly fearful ways by retreating from the problems of living, or by responding with extreme aggression to everyday circumstances. Social anxiety may prevent people from communicating and forming beneficial relationships. And some people have irrational fears and phobias, like a fear of small creatures, a fear of heights, a fear of failure, or fear future events.

## 5
## Proactive & Reactive Stress Management

The two most common stress management skills are reactive stress management and proactive stress management. Reactive stress management is how you manage your stress in the moment as you experience it. Stressful events often cause frustration, for example, when trying to resolve a difficult problem, or when something creates an obstacle that prevents progress. And that frustration can lead to anger and other emotions that create less than desirable outcomes. So, one stress management technique is to recognize that frustration, and reduce that frustration, or learn to respond to those frustrations differently. In fact, you have many options in terms of how you react to stress and frustration. Improving your ability to relax, objectively analyze your circumstances, and consider alternative approaches, can enable you to more effectively create positive outcomes.

Proactive stress management attempts to reduce stress by planning ahead, by taking breaks, reducing conflict, improving relationships, and planning your day. This involves structuring your life, attitude, and thinking to reduce foreseeable problems and maximize benefits. Ideally, you want to control the things you have control of. So, anything you have control over, like your productivity, learning, planning, problem solving, how you spend your time, could be proactively managed to reduce the amount of stress you would experience from not doing so.

Stress management experts recommend managing your time more effectively as a way to reduce unnecessary stress. For example, plan things out in advance to prevent unnecessary distress caused by being late for deadlines or missed appointments. Create realistic expectations, get enough sleep, develop satisfying relationships, and avoid too much confrontation and argument.[42]

## 6
## Positive Thinking

Positive thinking is the ability to bring about positive thoughts and emotions, which can help to reduce distress, prevent unwanted losses, and enable you to more effectively make wanted gains, in terms of health, productivity, and personal relationships. Positive thinking can be both a proactive and reactive stress management technique.

If you recognize negative thoughts and emotions before they quickly escalate, you may be able to return to positive thinking. Approaching your day, work, and personal relationships with positive thinking and a positive attitude, can lead to positive experiences and positive change in your life, relationships, and career. The positive energy that comes out of positive thinking can produce greater self-confidence, self-esteem, better health, better outcomes, and stronger relationships.

The negative energy and comes out of negative thinking can produce conflict, despair, negative outcomes, and weaker relationships. Breaking out of a negative state of mind can be difficult because negative circumstances often produce more negative thinking. For example, experiencing a significant loss in your life, or being the victim of another person's irresponsible or criminal actions. Positive thinking is not the same as pretending that problems do not exist, because those problems may continue to cause dissatisfaction, conflict, and other forms of negativity if those problems are not resolved.

But the inability to recover from a negative state of mind, can increase stress, anger, conflict, social avoidance, impulsive actions, or pessimism, which can harm your physical and mental health, productivity, property, and personal relationships. So, positive thinking, combined with other types of skills and abilities, can improve your overall health, wellbeing, and become a powerful tool it striving to be successful in achieving your life goals.

# 7
## Escapism

Escapism could be interpreted as escaping from the stresses of life, which could be as simple as watching entertainment or going on a nature walk. This is akin to the flight-response when avoiding the challenges of living. Avoiding difficulties for short periods of time can be beneficial. But too much avoidance can be harmful. First of all, you cannot avoid all of life's difficulties that cause distress, like work, personal relationships, or daily responsibilities. Avoiding these problems leaves them an unresolved and a potential ongoing source of dissatisfaction. But, at the same time, the stress from working long hours, especially negative stressors, can drain your energy and cause frustration, which can impair your thinking and judgment.

Taking a break can have a temporary positive effect on

your emotions and energy. A break, whether it is a ten-minute break or a vacation, can be recreational by helping you to recreate positive emotions, positive relationships, and a positive and healthy outlook. If you are angry about something, relaxation can enable you to recuperate your energy, and help you to experience fewer negative emotions when you return to work. All of these things can counter the negative effects of distress and can enable you to approach your work with renewed energy and optimism. The more you enjoy life, the more enjoyable life becomes. But if you spend too much time enjoying life, it could take time away from longer-term goals that would bring you satisfaction later in life.

8

Battles

Getting what you want sometimes requires confronting difficulties and fighting many small battles. If you want a beautiful garden, then you need to attack the weeds. Many of these small daily battles are not necessarily violent or emotional, but are more of a persistent effort to finish a project, or persuade a person to make one choice over another.

Ideally, you want to start battles you can win. So, you should choose your battles wisely. Some battles you can win, and some battles you will lose. And not all battles are worth fighting. Fighting a losing battle may not be in your best interest if doing so puts you in a worse situation, or causes other people significant harm. Fighting a losing battle can also cause tensions and emotions to escalate, which can impair your judgment and negatively influence decisions that can leave you worse-off.

How you approach you battles will determine your victories and losses. For example, if your boss proposes a new policy that you think will hurt the business, then screaming at your boss may not be the most effective approach to resolving that problem. If your boss sees you as behaving irrationally, your boss may stop being receptive and may not cooperate with you. Instead, you may be able to create a presentation that outlines the negative consequences of the policy, which may be more effective at influencing the outcome.

## 9
## Attitude & Tone

Attitude and tone when communicating with people can significantly influence stress levels, and the willingness to cooperate among everyone involved. And you will face difficulties that will create distress, anger, and frustration. And that distress can certainly influence your attitude and tone when communicating with people.

In business, management can get into the bad habit of only expressing blame toward workers, or criticizing worker performance for mistakes or failures, instead of figuring out the root causes of failure and fixing it. If management is incapable of working to resolve problems with workers, and continues to have low confidence in the people they depend on, those workers may not know what management expects. And instead, stress and conflict may increase among everyone involved. A more constructive approach would be to avoid blaming each other and instead try to figure out the cause of the problem and fix it.

For example, suppose Tim runs a software development business and one of his clients wants a refund because Tim's employees did not deliver the product in the agreed amount of time. Tim is angry. He sends out an email to his development team accusing them of being lazy, asking why he is paying them to lose clients, and threatening to fire people. Tim's email did not help the situation. When Tim confronted the team in person, he realized that his email created heightened tension among the team. When Tim asked the team why they lost a high-paying client, team members blamed each other. Rather than motivating the team to find a solution, it pitted team members against each other and made them fearful for their jobs. Upon reflecting on his email, Tim realized he was being too harsh and not constructive in helping his team resolve the problem that caused them to lose their client. He wrote another email thanking the team for their effort, and encouraged his team to continue to have a positive attitude. And later, Tim got with his development team to figure out what went wrong, so they could learn from their mistakes and prevent those mistakes from occurring in the future.

Allowing stress and life problems to influence your tone can directly influence people's behavior. Life problems can certainly put you into a terrible mood and grumpy attitude. But you have a choice about how to behave, and do not have to allow stress and life problems to influence how you treat people. If you constantly have a negative attitude or tone for some unknown reason, people may be less willing to offer you help.

10<br>State of Mind

Managing stress ultimately involves controlling your state of mind and what you attend to in the moment. You can change your state of mind by changing your cognitive focus, by engaging in different activities that stimulate different responses and evoke different emotions. If you are experiencing a significant amount of distress, engaging in different activities, like a hobby, can help you relax, maintain self-control, and prevent negative emotions that could influence your decision-making.

The most difficult part of controlling your state of mind has to do with forces beyond your control causing your distress. For example, other people will make decisions that will negatively impact your interests in some way. And that will certainly be angering, especially if you are not able to do anything about it. So, instead of ruminating in a pool of toxic anger, you could change your focus to projects you have more control over. Deeply involving yourself in a long-term project can change your focus from the moment you wake up, to the moment you go to sleep, so that you stop focusing on sources of stress entirely.

Changing your environment can be one of the most effective means of changing your state of mind. Consider a colleague of mine, Jerry, a software engineer who spends much of his day writing and debugging code. One day, he pounded on his desk and exclaimed: "What is wrong with this stupid thing!" He pounded keys on his keyboard, made frustrated grunts, and uttered annoyed remarks. He was trying to fix a bug in a program but did not know what was causing it. He thought the program should work, but for some unknown reason it did not. Jerry's stress and frustration only slowed him down as he threw fits and broke things. He called it a piece of crap and attacked the problem in all the wrong ways, which will not help him to solve the problem any quicker. After noticing Jerry's frustration, I asked him to join me for a game of Table Tennis in the recreation room. After a few sets, we were both happier and Jerry was smiling. Within a couple of minutes after returning, Jerry was able to figure out the problem that had stumped him.

Taking breaks during work can reduce distress that impairs thinking. Your brain and body both need rest during extended periods of activity. And research shows that when solving complex problems for an extended period of time, parts of the brain can grow tired, making it more difficult to solve those problems. So, taking a break every once-in-a-while allows the brain and body to recover so you can continue to be productive and effective in solving the problems you face.

Changing your environment so it produces pleasant emotions, and reduces distress, can also help. In the work environment, some managers attempt to do that by making the atmosphere fun or entertaining. Some people use meditation, or mindfulness, to develop impulse control and improve cognitive focus. When you meditate, you are trying to purge your restless mind of residual thoughts and emotions, usually by focusing only on breathing. After your mind is clears of all thoughts and emotions, you may be able to harness the power of positive thinking more effectively.

Simply finding time away from work related responsibilities for leisure, games, creative activities, or physical and mental recreation, can improve your emotional disposition, sense of wellbeing, and create positive memories. These experiences can help to reinforce a refreshed, positive, and optimistic outlook when you return to work.

# CHAPTER IX:
# TIME MANAGEMENT SKILLS

The last chapter briefly looked at how you spend your time can influence your stress levels. For example, you will experience more distress if you are constantly out of time and are never able to finish things. It can influence your personal development, if you never make time to develop the necessary skills to be more effective in your career. Your time management can influence your life satisfaction, if you never have time to achieve your goals. And this chapter looks at some strategies for managing your time more wisely.

## 1
## Time Management Techniques

*Time management* involves how you allocate the time on your schedule to pursue the things you want. The choices you make throughout the day have a huge influence on how your time is managed. If you are not thinking about time management, you may not be giving yourself enough time to achieve your goals, which could influence your life satisfaction. So, this section looks at a few techniques for effective time management.

Start with low-hanging fruit. Complete small, manageable, tasks that can be done right-way, especially those that you need to do. If you are working on a project that has a due date, get more work done sooner (e.g., preliminary brainstorming, research, and rough draft) to give yourself more time to improve the quality of the work and reduce stress about the pending deadline. Getting more work done earlier creates a time surplus, and gives you more time in the future to pursue the things you want.

Prioritize goals that are most important to you. As you grow older, you will accumulate more things you want to do. But as you put more goals in front of yourself, you accumulate more time deficits. Instead of getting ahead, you always find yourself falling behind. So, decide which goals you want to achieve now, and which goals can wait until later.

Make time for pursuing your goals. Making time is similar to making space. If you need space, you have two options: Move everything together or remove half the items. Time is similar in that you can work faster, or forego opportunities. Attempting to do everything at a breakneck speed is not the wisest time management strategy because it can lead to stress, mistakes, accidents, and poor decisions that were not thoroughly thought threw. Give yourself plenty of time to do high priority tasks. For example, if your employer expects you to be at work at a specific time, then give yourself plenty of time so you are not angry at slow drivers, stressed out, and late to work.

Lastly, make time for sufficient rest, sleep, and recreation. Logically, if you want to get more done, you need to spend more time being productive. That seems logical because if you do not put in enough effort, you never make progress, and your projects will develop very slowly. But, if you try to work too much, you may experience sleep deprivation, severe fatigue, and exhaustion, which can impair your brain's ability to function properly. You will see a decline in your ability to learn, pay attention, and in your judgement and decision-making abilities. To perform well, give your brain and body the optimal amount of rest and sleep.

2

Goal Setting

Leverage time to complete long-term, or difficult, tasks by breaking-up longer-term goals, which take months or years to complete, into smaller daily or weekly goals. Breaking-down large goals into smaller goals is the foundation for all developmental solutions, whether you are developing skills and following the Principle of Gradual Improvement, or working on a complex project.

Too often, people are impatient, and demand immediate results, which may not be realistic and may lead to failure. A time-consuming goal, like developing a skill, is a developmental process that requires a significant amount of time and effort. If you want to body-build and have never trained before, then starting with heaviest weights is an unrealistic expectation that could put you in the hospital. A more effective approach would be to start with smaller goals, like lifting smaller weights in sets of repetitions, and then slowly working up to heavier weights after you have developed the muscles to do so.

Breaking-down complex, or longer-term, goals into manageable, shorter-term, goals creates proximate goals, or milestones, that are more achievable. You can have greater confidence in your ability to achieve smaller, shorter-term, goals, rather than larger, more insurmountable goals. And since those goals are more achievable, they are more likely to pay off, and you are more capable of building a track record of success.

3

Productivity

*Productivity*, in Economics, is a measure of the amount of work performed, and specifically a measure of output, in terms of the amount of goods and services produced. Productivity, in your own life, may be measured by the amount of time and energy spent working towards achieving a goal. If you want to continue making gains toward achieving your life goals and create a more satisfying life, instead of squandering and wasting your opportunities, then you need to stay productive. Your life will never change, and you will never make progress towards obtaining the things you want, by procrastinating. The more you accomplish now, in terms of productivity, like repetitions of exercise, pages read, or weeds pulled from your garden, the more satisfied you will be with the final result.

The amount of effort put into achieving a goal has a profound influence on its success. The success of an effort usually does not hinge upon any single pivotal decision, but usually a series of decisions, a sustained effort, and a hard-fought march toward a desired end, in which you will make many mistakes, and experience significant gains and losses. While know-how certainly helps, and may be absolutely required in certain knowledge-based jobs, effort ultimately makes a project successful.

Human effort is one of the most influential success factors beyond the planning stage. Without enough effort, projects fail. So, as you work towards achieving a goal, you will face difficulties and make mistakes, which can be discouraging. And that discouragement could lead to giving-up. But as you learn from those mistakes, get better with practice, you can discover new approaches that will help you to be more successful the next time.

Effort also translates into the development of the skills required to be successful. For example, if Susan wants to be a winning athlete, but applies a strategy of showing up and trying her best, she will probably lose. To be competitive, she needs to practice, exercise, test her abilities, and measure her progress against those of other athletes. As she measures her performance against other athletes, she can create proximate goals that will gradually bring her performance closer to that of other athletes.

4
Creativity

*Creativity* is the ability to bring something new into the world. One way of being creative is by envisioning what is missing in a picture or arrangement and trying to fill-in that void. Gestalt psychology shows us that the human brain does this automatically as it fills-in the missing details of perception to create a more organized, meaningful, and complete mindscape of reality. People also do it in their deliberate thinking, when they draw from the palette of their interests to envision the lives they want, and what is required to turn that vision into reality. Much of this creative-urge comes from a perceived incompleteness, from appetites that need to be nourished, wants and goals that need to be achieved, voids that need to be filled, knowledge that needs to be learned, and problems that need to be solved.

The discovery process is often the first step in the creative process. After all, you cannot know what you have to work with until you discover it. Discoveries are sometimes made by playing with the materials you have, by adding to them, subtracting from them, changing them, replacing them, or recombining them in new patterns. Creativity can occur by fusing two ideas together to make something new.

Experimentation alone cannot guarantee that you, or anyone else, will be satisfied with the end result. As you acquire more experience, exposure, and knowledge, you acquire more examples of what works and does not work that can add to your expertise. By looking at what other people have done, or looking at how they have solved a similar problem, can help you to discover what works. You could talk to people, do research, seek new experiences, and discover new and different examples. If you want to remodel your living space, look at existing examples for ideas, and tailor those ideas to fit your needs by adding to them and innovating them. You could study successful projects, or seek education about what is already known. Studying existing work reduces the need for trial-and-error experimentation that is more likely to fail then it will succeed.

Modelling your creative process on paper before implementing your design can be tremendously helpful in studying, analyzing, and improving your design, before investing a significant amount of time and money on building it. You may want to create a list of features, enhancements, problems, and budget, before committing to the building process. This helps you to determine a project's viability, and enables you to create a realistic timeline for the completion of that project.

5
Choice Alternatives

Every decision you make has a tradeoff, or opportunity cost, which includes the opportunities you forego to get something in return. For example, if you want to live a healthier lifestyle, you may give-up junk food or spend time exercising. Or a Farmer in Oklahoma may consider whether it is more profitable to grow wheat or cotton this season. Or, suppose Tim is 16-years-old. And during the weekends, he has the opportunity to work at the restaurant around the corner, or he could play video games with his friends. Playing games will cost him the money he could earn at the restaurant. Alternatively, if he works at the restaurant, he could save enough money to buy transportation that would take him to a higher paying job. Pursuing one opportunity, can cost you other, potentially better, opportunities.

Life may not present you with the best opportunities. But you have more control over, and responsibility for, the choices you make and the opportunities you pursue than anything else in your life. You have the opportunity to be something, to be successful at something, to be great at what you do, or to create a more satisfying life. Think about the opportunities that are in front of you now. Which of those is the best opportunity? And if you are not pursuing that opportunity, then why? People often have great opportunities standing right in front of them that they fail to pursue. And the one ability that separates highly successful people from those who are not may be the ability to quickly recognize, and take advantage of, those opportunities, similar to how a successful entrepreneur takes advantage of a good business opportunity.

You can also use techniques to give yourself better opportunities. For example, to avoid too little opportunity, you could expand your options. This is may be necessary when you do not have enough options and begin to feel trapped in an undesirable situation where you have no choice in matters. That could lead to a feeling helplessness, like the learned helplessness introduced by Psychologist Martin Seligman of Positive Psychology, which was introduced in the first chapter. To overcome that helplessness, give yourself more options, find new opportunities, develop new skillsets, or develop new relationships. If Frank is considering moving to a new apartment, he could choose his first option. Or he may weigh the pros and cons between the first option, and the apartment next door. The problem with this scenario is that he is limiting himself to two options. Consequently, Fred maybe forcing himself to make a less-than-desirable decision when better alternatives exist. If he explores other possibilities, he may be able to find a more desirable alternative.

Economist Herbert Simon made the case that people have bounded rationality, in which they are limited in time, cognitive ability, and information. Because of these limitations, people are forced to accept satisfactory outcomes, rather than ideal outcomes. As people expand their options, they try to do one of two things: They choose the option that sufficiently meets their minimum requirements within the constraints of their limited means, which Simon called satisficing, or they choose the best option given their limited means, which is sometimes called optimizing. A Satisficer makes choices that sufficiently meets one's needs, while an Optimizer makes choices that gets the most out of what one has.

Whether people suffice or optimize depends on the

choice being made and whether that choice may result in a positive, negative, or inconsequential outcome. For example, if all shoes were equal in quality, then any pair of shoes would suffice. In that situation, you could go to the nearest discount store and purchase any pair of shoes that fits. And that would satisfice. Or you could optimize, shop around, and spend a little more money to purchase a pair that is comfortable, within your budget, and will last for a longer period of time.

This way of evaluating your options is also called Cost/Benefit Analysis, which is a formal management practice that studies how to maximize gains or minimize losses. Managers use many types of data models and formulas to analyze the costs and benefits of business decisions. But, in your private life, considering what you stand to gain or lose from a decision can prevent unwanted losses. People who are more successful in achieving their goals not only recognize great opportunities, they weigh the costs and benefits of those opportunities and pursue those that yield the greatest payoff.

In terms of options, having too many options can overwhelm you and cause you to make a random choice that results in a poor decision. So, once you have expanded your options, you need to limit, or narrow down, your options to the most desirable ones, to make your choice easier. You could stick only to opportunities that are consistent with your lifegoals. You could eliminate options that could have a negative impact on relationships or financial condition. Or, you could seek the advice of an expert who may be able to help you make an informed decision.

In their book *Nudge: Improving Decisions About Health, Wealth, and Happiness*, Richard Thaler and Cass Sunstein make a case for choice-architectures (i.e., arranging the environment to influence people's choices) to help people make decisions that are more aligned with their longer-term interests. An example of a choice architecture would be how certain items are strategically placed in checkout lanes in a Supermarket to influence buyer decisions. Candy will be strategically place in the checkout line because they know it will provoke child nagging, which may influence a parent's decision to purchase the candy.

Choice architectures, according to Thaler and Sunstein, could help people make better choices, especially younger people who are unwilling to spend money on health insurance or a retirement savings account. People are loss averse, they argue, and are motivated more by the fear of loss than they are by the prospect of gains. Younger adults have little motivation to put the small amount of money they earn in a retirement fund. So, Thaler and Sunstein suggest employers could provide a default option, which would automatically enroll employees in a retirement fund. Employees would, then, be allowed to opt out, if they choose.[56]

Adding default options to contractual agreements and the technologies we use, makes life easier, and could certainly improve decision-making. But default options cannot be added to every choice people make. Thaler and Sunstein acknowledged that much and add that, unfortunately, people are nudged into decisions that are not in their best interests but are, instead, in the interests of other people. Businesses are notorious for creating default options that play into their profit margins by making false promises, or taking advantage of unsuspecting buyers.

6

## Risk Mitigation

Risk-mitigation is an attempt to reduce the severity of losses, which is not the same as risk-avoidance or risk-aversion. Risk is in everything you do. As you strive to obtain what you want in life, whether in your relationships, employment, or traveling, you face uncertainty and the risk of loss or failure. If you try something new, you risk failing. In every business transaction, the buyer or seller risks losing money. So, achieving your goals and creating the life you want, requires a certain amount of risk tolerance, and the ability to mitigate that risk. This section looks at some techniques for risk mitigation.

The first of these is to avoid being too risk averse when engaging in the activities necessary to achieve goals. People may be risk averse because of inexperience that could lead to failure. Achieving goals requires stepping out of your comfort zone, and at times experiencing loss and failure. You may fail in your job, or may be rejected in your relationships. And you may be judged based on those successes or failures. But if you do not accept some risk of loss or failure in pursuit of your goals, you will never succeed.

The second is to avoid unnecessary risks. If you expose yourself to too much risk, you could face unnecessary and devastating consequences. For example, every time you drive to work, you risk getting into an accident. That is a normal risk. But some drivers drive too close to over vehicles, increasing their likelihood of getting into a serious accident. In the event that an unexpected obstruction ends up in the lane, those drivers are not providing themselves or other motorists with enough time to stop, which guarantees a life-threatening accident. Since that risk is easily avoidable, it is an unnecessary risk.

Contrary to popular beliefs, big risks do not necessarily mean big rewards. Quitting your job and getting a loan to finance a restaurant is certainly a big risk and could eventually lead to big rewards. But if you lack a clear vision, a solid business plan, a viable product, or lack knowledge about the local market or the restaurant industry, your restaurant may never make enough money and you may end up in bankruptcy. Entrepreneurship, like all other life endeavors, involves risk. But you have to learn how to mitigate those risks with know-how and effort to improve certainty in success.

Make decisions based on what you know for certain. If you want to build a restaurant, you need more than just a belief it will succeed. You need to create and test a menu, figure out where you are going to source your ingredients, and calculate how much to charge to cover all your operating costs. These are all things you can know beforehand. And you can use that knowledge to determine whether you have a viable business model before taking the giant leap and establishing your business. Or it could help you determine whether you need to improve and refine your business model, to improve certainty of success.

Create realistic goals that you know you can achieve. That could start by creating realistic expectations in your time and budget estimates. People are impatient and sometimes create unrealistic expectations for themselves or other people. If you try to complete a time-consuming task in an unrealistically short period of time, you are likely to give-up and fail. One way of making your goals and time estimates more realistic is by padding your margins. Slightly overestimating the amount of time or money required to finish a project can help you avoid time or budget overruns. If your morning commute normally takes 20 minutes, then plan for a 30-minute commute to account for unforeseen delays. Or if a work-related project takes three weeks to complete, then plan to work on it for four weeks to allow for unforeseen events and challenges that will inevitably arise. Or when making capacity planning decisions, planners sometimes budget for slightly more capacity than what is required to avoid falling short and making costly mistakes. In the end, you, and other people, will be more satisfied with your work as you deliver on your promises on a more consistent basis.

And lastly, avoid ventures that depend entirely on luck and chance, especially when the probability of achieving your desired goal is low. Gambling and the Lottery are considered entertainment, not a retirement plan. If a decision results in one of two possible outcomes, then the probability of achieving your goal is the same as a coin flip, which is close 50 percent. As you increase the number of possible outcomes, assuming the result depends on chance, the probability of success in achieving the goal goes down, and the probability of failure goes up. If your chance of winning the Lottery is 1-in-175 million, then putting all of your savings into lottery tickets may not be the soundest financial plan. Hoping something will happen, and making decisions based on wishful thinking, will not be as successful as making decisions based on what you know for certain.

# CHAPTER X:
# MENTAL DISORDERS

A *mental disorder* is an abnormal mental condition that disrupts, impairs, or interferes with the normal function or development of human abilities. Most mental disorders are common and completely harmless. Some types of mental disorders are so severe, they cause mental health problems. If you do not have a mental disorder yourself, then you probably know someone who does, whether it is a family member, a spouse, a manager, or a child. And this chapter can help you to recognize and handle those disorders.

Mental disorders do not include common stressors, religious rituals, socially accepted religious beliefs, social deviance, societal conflicts, or cultural conflicts. But a mental condition that causes a person to be inconsolably sad for unknown reasons, or a mental condition that causes a person to be extremely hostile for unknown reasons, is indicative of a mental disorder. Some examples include phobias, irrational fears, hallucinations, delusions, obsessions, uncontrollable rage, and inconsolably sadness. A person with a mental disorder may see a harmless person as evil, or may see their own life as hopeless and meaningless. All of these perceptions result from abnormal development or abnormal function of a person's cognitive abilities.

1
The Impact of Mental Disorders

Previous chapters looked at how to strengthen cognitive abilities to improve your mental condition, mental health, and your outlook on life. Mental disorders, in contrast, result from the abnormal development or abnormal function of cognitive abilities. A study by the United States Department of Health and Human Services found that "mental and behavioral disorders and serious emotional disturbances (SEDs) in children and adolescents can lead to school failure, alcohol or illicit drug use, violence, or suicide." Among people age 65 and older, an estimated 25 percent, or "(8.6 million) experience specific mental disorders, such as depression, anxiety, substance abuse, and dementia, that are not part of normal aging." Only 2.6 to 2.8 percent of adults in the United States suffer from the most severe and debilitating disorders. And the majority of people with mental disorders neglect to seek help.

The HHS study found that untreated mental disorders cost in terms of "lost productivity due to illness, premature death, criminal justice interaction process, and property loss." During 1996, for example, almost $70 billion was spent in the United States treating and diagnosing mental disorders. Nearly $75 billion more was spent on disability insurance and lost productivity because of illness or deaths that were attributed to mental disorders. And another $6 billion was spent on property loss, law enforcement, and criminal justice because of mental disorders that same year.[15]

2

Severity of Mental Disorders

The Diagnostic and Statistical Manual of Mental Disorders (DSM) lists over 400 types of mental disorders. But the most common are anxiety disorders, which, according to the United States Department of Health and Human Services, are known to affect nearly one out of four people in the United States in a given year.[15] A few of those include phobias, mood disorders, panic disorder, obsessive compulsive disorder, social anxiety disorder, generalized anxiety disorder, or posttraumatic stress disorder. These conditions are harmless, common, and do not prevent people from being productive, engaging in healthy relationships, or discharging emotions in socially acceptable ways.

If we compared a phobia to a physical illness, it would be comparable to an allergy. Having a fear of heights, dark places, spiders, snakes, small spaces, isolation, or loneliness is like being allergic to those things. And those fears are rational, to some extent, because it is true that you could fall to your death, get bit by an insect and get sick, or drowned in water. Those tendencies are part of how people protect themselves from the dangers of living to ensure their survival. So mental health and wellness is not considered to be attributed to the absence of mental disorders, like phobias, mental allergens, or other mild mental disorders that are common among people.

Mental disorders also tend to be confused with mental health problems. But mental health is not attributed to the absence of mental disorders. In fact, a person could have one or more mental disorders and have no symptom of a mental health problem. But if a mental disorder is severe enough, it can cause a decline in mental health if it leads to problems with behaving responsibly, substance abuse, abusive behaviors, or crime.

A severe mental disorder can prevent a person from functioning normally and making decisions that are in one's best interests. A person with a severe form of depression, for example, may have less confidence in one's abilities, greater self-doubt, greater despair, and may be more likely to give-up and throw away positive life opportunities. And that may cause a person to think about suicide more frequently. A person with a severe mental disorder may be overwhelmed with emotions, have distorted perceptions, and false beliefs, which can interfere with that person's ability to operate normally and interact with people.

The main difference between a mental disorder and a mental health problem (i.e., a mental illness) is that an illness usually threatens to harm a person or other people as a result of the person's mental state and behavior, for example, as a result of neglecting responsibilities, drug abuse, or threatening behaviors. The most extreme symptoms of mental disorders can lead to hospitalization, incarceration, or homelessness. A mental disorder that is severe enough to threaten a person (e.g., suicidal tendencies), or other people (e.g. homicidal tendencies), is usually considered to be a mental illness requiring mental health treatment. Mental illnesses often result in public order crimes, or other types of crimes, where law enforcement officers may be required to intervene. And if an offender is incarcerated, and the inmate does not receive treatment, the inmate's condition could worsen before being released back into the public.

3

## Causes of Mental Disorders

Mental disorders have many root causes, some of which are caused by a biological abnormalities or abnormal cognitive development. Mental disorders can result from genetic, neurological, biochemical, and anatomical abnormalities, like brain tumors. Mental disorders are sometimes attributed to biological differences that can only be corrected with prescription drugs. But if the mental disorder is the result of abnormal cognitive development instead of biological differences, then that diagnosis is not only wrong, but could actually prevent the patient from getting better. Ending medication without seeking professional advice is never recommended. But, in many cases, it's possible that medication may treat the short-term symptoms while the patient works on a longer-term developmental solution.

In the first chapter, we looked at how a person's mental development can be precluded by situational factors. When a person is told early in life that one is not good enough, or smart enough, to do well, it reduces that person's self-confidence, and confidence in one's abilities to overcome the difficulties of life, which leads to despairing and giving-up. Severe harsh treatment in an abusive relationship, or child abuse or neglect, can interfere normal mental development and cause emotional disorders, substance use, suicidal tendencies, and law enforcement intervention. Developing a habit of responding with extreme aggression or sadness can strengthen, and become increasingly hardwired and fixed overtime, so that it becomes more like a mental disorder. Or traumatic brain injury caused by high impact sports, or explosions in combat or military training, can cause mental disorders, like Post Traumatic Stress Disorder.

Conditioning, which is a process of developing responses as a result of repeated reinforcement, provides some evidence for how phobias and irrational fears develop as a result of positive or negative association with specific types of things. Some of the earliest experiments in Conditioning, or what is now called Classical Conditioning, were conducted by Ivan Pavlov during the late 19th century. His experiments demonstrated how a neural stimulus could be conditioned to produce an involuntary reflex. In one experiment, he associated the sound of a metronome with food, which caused a dog to salivate when presented with the sound of the metronome.

In the early decades of the 20th century, John Watson and Rosalie Rayner purportedly conditioned an eleven-month-old child to fear animals. The child, who they called Albert, was introduced to a rat, rabbit, and a monkey, which were the neutral stimuli in the experiment. At first, Albert was unafraid, curious, and wanted to touch the animals. When the researchers surprised Albert by striking a steel bat with a hammer (i.e., the unconditioned stimulus) he began to cry. When the researchers combined the two in repeated experiments, and struck the bat in the presence of a rat, Albert's fear of the sound transferred to the rat. In other words, Albert learned to fear the rat. When researchers presented the rat without the sound, Albert would cry and crawl away. Albert's fear also transferred to other animals and developed into a generalized phobia of other small animals, an effect they called stimulus generalization. Consequently, any animal caused Albert to cry and crawl away.[29] Watson and Raynor later suggested that this type of conditioning could influence a person's behavior long after the events occurred.[62]

These experiments in conditioning have provided some

evidence for how likes, dislikes, loves, and fears, can develop as a result of life experiences and routine circumstances. If those fears were purely anatomical, purely formed by biology without the influence of experience, then you would expect a person with a phobia to have greater than average fear in general. But you can find many instances where that is not the case. For example, a tight-rope walker who is afraid of spiders. Or a crocodile wrangler who is afraid of heights. People see danger in snakes when others do not. And a harmless comment may appear malicious. So, fears tend to be localized to very specific things.

Since many disorders, like phobias, may be the result of abnormal cognitive development, they might be corrected over a period of time using developmental solutions. For example, strengthening social or occupational abilities can improve self-confidence, and a person's outlook on life. Developing new skills can rewire the brain to think differently. But developmental solutions, like that, require a considerable amount of time and effort, and trust in the final solution.

4

Depression

According to a Department of Health and Human Services report, during one year alone, depression cost the United States $40 billion due to lost productivity and health care costs, making it a "leading cause of absenteeism and diminished productivity" in the workplace.[15] People are more likely to experience depression when they are distressed, pessimistic, have a low self-worth, or have a medical condition, like cancer, stroke, or a hormonal disorder. Extreme life changes requiring significant adjustment, like unem-

ployment, as well as financial problems, problematic relationships, and significant losses, are also causes of depression.[46]

In the first chapter, we looked at studies conducted by
Psychologists Martin Seligman and Steven Maier during the
1960's on learned helplessness, whereby people may learn
to feel helpless as a result of lacking control over life circumstances. Seligman later suggested that learned helplessness
could explain depression in people.[28] The extent to which
learned helplessness develops in people is unknown. A person who is in an abusive relationship, like a child who is
unable to escape the daily mistreatment of an abusive parent, may develop learned helplessness. Or a person trapped
in miserable and impoverished circumstances, like living in
a high-crime community where one can barely afford a living wage, may be more susceptible to feeling helpless,
which would influence that person's outlook on life.

## 5
## Schizophrenia

Schizophrenia influences judgment, decision-making, and
life outcomes as a result of altered cognitive processes, perceptions, speech, and emotions. The disorder is rare and is
known to affect about one percent of the population in the
United States. Those who suffer hear voices, hallucinate,
and have false beliefs, and other symptoms that come and
go. At times an affected person may see, smell, or feel things
that are not present, like the nervous system is sending false
signals to the brain.

Symptoms include delusions that others are trying to
control one's thoughts through brain or radio waves, or periods of disorganized thinking where a person's speech has

no logical meaning, or the individual has a hard time completing sentences, or makes up words. People with schizophrenia often have problems with memory, attention span, personal hygiene, and problems making decisions based on facts and reality. All of these can prevent a person from earning a living or have normal relationships. Studies show that people with schizophrenia are more likely to attempt suicide. And about 10 percent of those that try actually succeed.[47]

6

Substance Use Disorder

Substance use disorder, or substance abuse, is a mental disorder characterized by the uncontrollable consumption of an intoxicating substance that leads to a variety of health, legal, and financial problems. Responsible substance use means understanding the consequences of using that substance. For example, a person may not consider the consequences of using a substance when one should be productive in work or social life. Or a person may not consider the consequences of how driving a vehicle when intoxicated increases the likelihood of causing an accident. Both of those are examples of not using a substance responsibly.

Since substance use impairs a person's normal mental function, it also impairs a person's ability to perform life roles and achieve certain goals. One of the most effective ways of preventing the negative consequences of substance use is by abstaining, having a fully sober day, or consuming a small enough quantity so that it does not affect you. Ideally people would have a fully sober day from the time they wake up to the time they go to sleep, so they can be fully productive in developing their skills and mental abilities, and so it does not interfere with their employment or social life. When people consume alcohol to entertain, they usually have rules for their consumption so they do not consume too much, like having a couple of beers during a two-hour period. But when a person uses a substance too much, too often, it can interfere with the performance of life roles and other responsibilities.

The cumulative side-effect of substance addiction is that the more a person uses an intoxicating substance, the less control that person has over one's life and how one is viewed or treated by other people. The negative side-effects of substance use could happen suddenly, like being arrested for committing a crime while intoxicated. Or, the negative side effects may accumulate slowly over a period of weeks, months, or years. Some are more obvious than others. For example, the U.S. Department of Health and Human Services says that impaired thinking caused by substance use leads to drownings, crimes, imprisonment, and death, and leads to hospital bills from emergency room visits, long-term healthcare costs, and rehabilitation costs.[16]

Excessive substance use, like alcohol consumption, can alter a person's physical appearance and behavior, even when sober. These side-effects create problems in relationships and employment, reduce personal and employment opportunities, and subject a person to lower wages. Impaired thinking caused by substance abuse has a negative influence on decision-making, memory, learning, personal development, and overall performance. The prolonged effects of intoxication may lead to social avoidance, the inability to perform work related responsibilities, and a decline in self-confidence, all of which makes a person more vulnerable to verbal attacks and criticism and leads to defensiveness, insecurity, and a sense of constantly being under attack. When a manager sees an employee who behaves, or looks hung-over, or is behaving irresponsible for unknown reasons, confidence in that person's abilities may decline. Managers may not employ, or promote, people who they suspect are abusing substances.

Many theories exist for how substance use disorders develop. Some addicts report having some type of chemical dependence, like using the substance to medicate an emotional or mental disorder, or using it for other reasons. A study published in the New England Journal of Medicine by Nora Volkow, George Koob, and A. Thomas McLellan researched substance addiction in the United States to gain a better understanding the addiction cycle. For simplicity, their research divided the substance dependence cycle into three stages: 1) binging and intoxication; 2) withdrawal and negative affects; and 3) preoccupation and anticipation.

In the first stage, the user views the experience produced by binging and intoxication as a reward. And the greater the perceived reward, the greater number of harmful consequences the user maybe willing to tolerate to engage in the activity. Because the substance alters brain chemistry with extended use, the user experiences withdrawal and the negative affect stage of the addiction cycle when the user is no longer intoxicated. During the withdrawal stage dopamine levels decrease, reward circuits are desensitized, and stress reactions grow stronger. In the last stage of the cycle, these changes in brain function cause the user to become preoccupied, and anticipate, the consumption of the substance. And despite the user's desire to quit, or the potential for devastating consequences, the user continues using the substance.[61]

The addiction cycle shows why people become trapped

by addictions. They not only anticipate the reward of intoxication, but feel insecurity about the negative effects of not using it. The user begins to depend on the substance to avoid withdrawal symptoms that may include severe stress reactions, a loss of sleep, tiredness, fatigue, absent mindedness, or could be as severe as hallucinations and seizures, depending on the substance.[21] The withdrawal symptoms become a source of worry and anxiety, so that not using the substance creates a perception of insecurity and risk.

Treatment for substance dependence can come from a variety of sources. Part of the problem is that people with addictions are sometimes punished by family members, or members of the community, who may believe that the harsh treatment will deter the person from doing it again. And that creates more distress and another excuse to depend on the substance to get through difficult times. Addicts may also be able to find needed help by joining a support group where members understand the problems of addiction and are willing to provide assistance and long-term help. Some help is better than no help. And seeking the help of a professional Therapist or support group can be a first step in resolving those problems.

Professional services can accelerate the resolution of the addiction before it has adverse effects and does more damage. Some substance abuse and rehabilitation clinics diagnose and attempt to treat the underlying triggers of the addiction, like mental or emotional disorders that trigger substance use. In addition, some teach life skills, like stress management, personal skills, leadership, and financial management, which can prevent a relapse by enabling the patient to more effectively handle life difficulties. In addition to these solutions, people should consider longer-term developmental solutions, like creating a life vision and pursuing life goals, that gives a person's life greater meaning and purpose, and a reason to have a fully sober and productive day.

7

## Recognizing a Mental Health Problem

A person with a mild mental disorder, like a phobia, or anxiety disorder, does not have a mental health problem and may live a very healthy and productive life. But a person with a severe mental disorder that threatens the person's wellbeing, or that of other people, is symptomatic of a mental health problem. For example, violent behaviors, or the inability to support oneself, as a result of one or more mental disorders are indicative of mental health problems that can lead to incarceration or death.

When we look at how mental health is defined by the U.S. Department of Health and Human Services, and how healthy people "cope with the stresses of life" and are able to "be productive," we could see how not being able to do those things could threaten a person's livelihood. A severe mental disorder, like severe depression, may prevent a person from being emotionally stable enough, or emotionally positive enough, to engage in normal daily activities.

A study by the Department of Health and Human Services during the year 2000, concluded that about 90 percent of all suicides were due to mental disorders, substance abuse, or a combination of both.[15]

Studies by the National Center for Injury Prevention and Control identified some risk factors for suicide, which include substance abuse, hopelessness, impulsivity, substantial social or economic losses, and physical illness.[45] Their studies also suggest that the reason young people feel the need to commit suicide is that they are overwhelmed by stress and depression and find suicide to be a solution to their problems. And in 2001, people over the age of 65 who committed suicide were diagnosed with moderate depression, a physical illness, or were divorced or widowed.[45]

# 8
## Developmental Solutions

Mental health problems may be the result of abnormal development that may involve biological factors or cognitive development. In either case, developmental solutions that further develop a person's skills or abilities can be beneficial for improving that person's self-confidence and outlook on life. But a person who is working toward developmental solutions must be aware that they require a significant amount of time, effort, and trust in the effectiveness of the solution.

People who have mental health problems often lack abilities that are characteristic of healthy people. For example, a person with a mental health problem may lack the ability to manage stress, take responsibility, develop healthy relationships, or use sound judgment. Each of these abilities are characteristic of mental health. And, if strengthened, those abilities could enable a person to live a very different and productive life, and enable a person to gain enough confidence in one's abilities to take on life difficulties and be more resilient during difficult times.

Anyone can apply developmental solutions as they do not require special medications or treatment. The only cost involved is time and effort, and the willingness to trust the end result. Trusting the end result, by itself, is sometimes the most difficult part of a developmental solution since the patient may have severe mental or biochemical abnormalities that have developed from chemical dependencies or frequent emotional states. As a person develops and strengthens abilities that are characteristic of mental health, the result should be increased confidence in one's abilities, greater responsibility for one's life and future, and an improved outlook on life.

# CHAPTER XI:
## SOCIAL RESPONSIBILITY

In an earlier chapter we looked at how responsibility is the ability to take ownership for the consequences of a decision. And when the consequences have an impact on a community or the environment, it is sometimes called social responsibility. Responsible public policy, for example, is policy that considers the consequences of a policy, in terms of how it impacts people lives, businesses, and the economy. The problem with that in many Democratic societies on a national and state level is that the consequences of those policies is rarely studied. Lawmakers propose solutions that seem reasonable often without consulting with experts or researchers on the potential repercussions (i.e., negative consequences).

This chapter looks at different forms of social responsibility, and why decision-makers, even in high-impact positions, have difficulty understanding the consequences of decisions. And that is especially true for complex decisions, like the creation of public policy that would have unknown repercussions on the local economies, governmental funding, private businesses, and the wellbeing of citizens.

1

# The Meaning of Social Responsibility

Social responsibility refers to the impact that decisions have on the people of a community, or the decision-maker as a member of a community. Different forms of social responsibility permeate throughout our society in unexpected ways. Even art, love, and spirituality, has some impact on people (even if purely emotional) and, therefore, ascribes attribution and responsibility to the creator. Even traditional principles, like the Golden Rule (i.e., treating people the way you would like to be treated), promotes socially responsible behavior as it helps people to consider how their decisions effect other people's lives. Political movements, like the Civil Rights movement in the United States, promoted socially responsible policies to reduce unfair losses, unfair treatment, and to make society more just and civilized for everyone.

In business, social responsibility is sometimes referred to as Corporate Social Responsibility and focuses on the impact that business operations have on communities or the environment. Business can certainly have a positive impact on communities by creating better products that improve people's lives, or increase profits and sales that put people to work and improve the standard of living. And in government, law makers are able to create public policies that make communities safer and a better place to live, or design public infrastructure projects that provide the means for economic growth.

But the decisions of managers or policy makers can also, inadvertently, have a detrimental impact on communities or the environment. For example, a business manager could decide to dispose of toxic waste irresponsibly, by pouring the chemicals into a river. And government officials may simply allow those actions to occur.

2

Environmental Responsibility

Modern technologies have certainly created more life satisfaction as a result of improving people's standard of living by making life easier and more convenient, or improving quality of life by providing people with clean water and electricity for refrigeration. But modern production and consumption have also resulted in many repercussions not considered when these modern systems were first created.

Economists call these repercussions negative externalities, which is pollution that is considered a cost of doing business that taxpayers agree to pay for. For example, waste that continues to fill-up landfills with plastics, one-time-use packaging, toxic waste, and metals. This is certainly a problem that presents opportunities for solutions as people are not only capable of consuming and polluting the environment, but bio-engineering ecosystems and terraforming it as well. The question is: Will scientists, technologists, and business, be able to create products that are not only good for human life, but good for the planet as well, by using materials that are more biodegradable or recyclable?

Consider the increasing the use of nitrogen fertilizers that, in addition to light and water, are essential for food production. In recent decades, some farms using nitrogen fertilizers have caused algae blooms (i.e., microscopic organisms that grow in water). The result of algae consuming oxygen and nutrients is that some lakes and oceans have "dead zones" because it kills fish, and other marine life, harvested by fisheries. So, how do farmers fertilize responsibly, in a way that considers the potential consequences of fertilizing and how it effects downstream farms and fisheries?

In the United States, this problem is usually remedied by government policies that try to incentivize businesses and organizations to be more socially or environmentally responsible by imposing fines for operations that have a negative impact on citizens or the environment.

## 3
## Public Goods & Services

Governments often try to act in the public's interests by providing public goods and services that improve communities and their economies, along with the life satisfaction of citizens. For example, public services may include police departments, fire departments, policy enforcement, and military protection. Some public goods are designed improve quality of life in communities by providing clean water, or environmental regulations designed to maintain healthy living conditions. Some public goods are designed to improve the standard of living by building roads and bridges upon which to transport materials for the construction of housing, manufacturing facilities, and office buildings, for the production and distribution of private goods and services.

Predicting the impact that government policies have on communities and local economies, and how they impact citizens, organizations, and businesses, can be challenging. In democratic societies, policy decisions are, ideally, influenced by private entities, like citizens and businesses, in addition to scientists and experts who may advise on the social and economic repercussions of a policy.

But a Lawmaker's policy decisions may also be heavily

influenced by intuition, financial or political interests, social biases and beliefs, and political affiliations. Policy decisions based purely on these criteria, without supporting evidence or the cooperation of experts, have unknown, and unintended, consequences for communities. Anyone can look at a problem, propose a solution, and provide supporting evidence for the effectiveness of that solution. And while those solutions may have a marginal public benefit, they may also have unknown and unintended negative consequences. For example, mandating that everyone purchase healthcare insurance may sound like a great idea until the people you are trying to help are unable to afford it.

Deciding which public policies and programs to finance can be equally challenging since governments have limited funding from taxpayer revenue and government issued bonds. Government spending can accumulate debt that, if not well managed, could threaten bankruptcy. At the same time, if government officials fail to sufficiently fund public goods and services, they stand the chance of neglecting to provide adequate services, or failing to protect citizens.

Not only do public officials need to consider these time and budgetary constraints to have an efficient and well-managed government, they need to apply critical thinking skills, and consult with experts, to understand the effects of complex policy decisions. Anyone could judge the safety of a bridge by using their intuition. But that intuition may not be enough to recognize whether the bride would collapse and kill more than a dozen people, or injure more than 140, as the I-35 Bridge collapse did during 2007. You could also make an intuitive judgment about the safety of a water source, as Michigan officials did in 2014, when they switched Flint's water supply to a different water source, contaminating the drinking water with high levels of lead and other heavy metals, causing serious health problems in residents of effected communities. Government officials, no doubt, have good intentions. But good intentions are not enough to produce responsible policies, or prevent predictable problems that kill or seriously injure people.

4

Reducing Social Problems

*Social problems* are those that have a detrimental impact on communities or the environment, like crime, substance abuse, personal mistreatment, mass-shootings, pollution, homelessness and other problems. And Lawmakers draft public policy to reduce many of these social problems. For example, criminal justice policies are designed to disincentivize criminal behavior by making sure people who victimize other people, or cause unfair losses, are removed from the public or deterred from engaging in those behaviors. And most people are incentivized to comply with the law because it provides, what an Economist may call a Penalty Avoidance Benefit, which is the benefit an entity, such as a person or business, receives from operating in accordance with laws and regulations.[52] Many of those benefits include money, freedom, additional liberties, additional protections, and certain advantages in the marketplace where a criminal record could put a person at a disadvantage. Violating legal prohibitions makes a person more susceptible to avoidable fines, prosecution, and incarceration. And the offender may be subject to greater intolerance and discrimination, depending on the nature of the crime.

Everyone wants law enforcement to protect them, and keep their community safe, from those who would do harm.

But law enforcement, alone, only goes so far in being a re-active form of crime reduction that does nothing to resolve the underlying thinking and behavioral problems that mo-tivate criminal behaviors in the first place. Reducing crimi-nal behaviors involves changing the thinking and root causes of behavior, which may include intellectual skills de-ficiencies or mental disorders. Until social programs are de-signed to address these underlying issues, the public has no way of preventing them from occurring, and no guarantee that when inmates are released from State custody, they will behave any differently. And that creates additional burdens on citizens, communities, and governmental agencies, in terms of constrained tax revenues, broken families, home-lessness, unemployment, repeat offenders, and other esca-lating problems.

Arguably, the State owes a duty of care to the public to provide inmates with treatment before they are released back into the public so they do not continue to endanger the community. If the State does not provide that duty of care, then you should have no reason to expect any change in an inmate's behavior. Creating an effective program can also be problematic if the root causes of criminal behaviors are not addressed, or programs do not continue to develop and become more effective over time.

Incarceration, by itself, does nothing help the underlying behavioral, emotional, or mental problems that resulted in a substance use, anger issues, theft, or other correctable be-haviors. People with those issues not only have difficulty behaving responsibility, they often do not care about the consequences of their decisions, or how they negatively im-pact people's lives. And when inmates are released from prison, they may be psychologically worse off when you

consider the stigma of a criminal conviction, difficulty finding employment, and a greater potential for dependence on
State services.

These problems may not be eradicated completely. But
with effort, they can certainly be reduced to a manageable
level, which provides a number of benefits to the citizens, in
terms of increasing community wealth, living standards,
and public satisfaction. The State would have a smaller
prison population, it would reduce incarceration related
taxpayer expenses, and it would enable States to afford
more effective rehabilitation programs. With a smaller
prison population, tax revenues would increase as a result
of increasing the number of taxpayers able to contribute to
economic wealth, and decreasing taxpayer burdens of housing inmates. The additional money going into the economy
could be used to benefit other areas of the community, like
education and training, recreation, and building safer
spaces.

5

Unintended Consequences

During the past 20 years, policy makers in the Unites States
have passed laws based on the theory that imposing harsher
sentences will reduce crime. Many politicians who sought
election led campaigns focused on appealing to voter biases
by promising to enact get-tough-on-crime laws designed to
increase offender's sentences, and mandatory sentencing
laws that mandate a minimum sentence for certain offences.
As a result of increasing the severity of punishments, States
have built more prisons to house more inmates, which has
resulted in one of the highest incarcerations rates in the
world. The consequence of those policies is that many States

have redirected tax revenues to finance the incarceration of inmates, which has caused financial shortages in State agencies and programs. And those financial shortages have caused systemic problems that have trickled down to cause other social problems.

Clearly, get-tough-on-crime laws and mandatory sentencing laws did not fully consider the repercussions those policies have on communities, governmental organizations, or private citizens. In Oklahoma, for example, repeat offenders of Misdemeanor crimes are labeled Felons and, in some cases, are required to spend years in prison. Misdemeanor crimes are considered minor petty offenses punishable by fines instead of incarceration. Felonies are more severe crimes that may be punishable by incarceration lasting for more than one year, or punishable by death. In addition to fines or incarceration, Felons may lose rights as citizens, like the right to serve on a jury, the right to own a fire arm, the right to vote, and the right to practice certain professions.

Added to the labeling are people's beliefs about that labeling. A criminal justice worker may know the difference between a first-degree and third-degree felony. But a Human Resources person only knows a Felon as a person who victimized another person by committing rape or murder. Felons tend to be portrayed in television dramas, movies, and the news as hardened career criminals that victimize people and should never be given a second chance. And that may be the mental model that most average people have of a Felon, without any distinction between a Capital Offense, like murder, and a victimless Misdemeanor traffic ticket.

Harsher labeling and sentencing also has significant economics costs. Consider a case in 1995, shortly after the State of California enacted a three-strikes law, a man was sentenced to 25-years to life for stealing a slice of pizza from some children. Officials in California later recognized those laws as extreme and revised them to include only violent offenders. But more recently in 2016, a man was arrested in Louisiana for stealing about $30 worth of candy bars. Having more than two convictions for shoplifting is a Felony in Louisiana, which at the time was a state having one of the highest incarceration rates in the world. Because he had prior non-violent convictions for shoplifting, he faced 20 years to life.

In those cases, the District Attorney may influence the defendant's charges. But once the defendant is charged, the presiding judge has little discretion in changing the punishment because of mandatory sentencing laws. The cost of incarceration to the State of Louisiana, at the time, was about $18 thousand dollars per year and about $360 thousand dollars over a 20-year period to imprison someone for stealing about $30 worth of candy bars.[2]

As States continued to incarcerate inmates, the cost to taxpayers continued to increase. Government agencies and taxpayers continue to increase the amount of spending on police protection, law enforcement, criminal justice, and other programs to mitigate the impact of social problems on communities. In some circumstances, like in Louisiana, that effort overwhelmed the criminal justice system, which resulted in convicting innocent people, or freeing violent offenders, due to the inability to properly process offenders. Other states saw prison overcrowding and a shortage of prison guards.

From an economic perspective, these policies present opportunity costs. When taxpayers spend an increasing amount of money incarcerating people, they forgo the opportunity to finance other public goods, like education, public safety, or public infrastructure, which may help to reduce crime and improve social conditions. That money could be spent removing urban decay, like abandon buildings that may be occupied by vagrants or criminals. It could be spent improving urban life and creating programs that give young people opportunities to develop skills and have positive experiences.

During 2017, Oklahoma, a state that had the second highest incarceration rate in the United States, housed over 61 thousand inmates. If the prison population were a city during that year, it would be the seventh largest city in Oklahoma. Despite having a budget shortfall of about $1 billion, the State was expected to spend $2 billion more to incarcerate people, forcing cities to close and consolidate schools.[23] The budget shortfall also created a teacher shortage due to having some of the lowest paid teachers in the United States forcing schools to issue 14 hundred emergency teaching certifications, which was a 10% increase over the previous year.[48]

Evidence suggests that these laws also have a detrimental impact on the lives of citizens. During 2014, Oklahoma had about 44 thousand homeless children, one of the highest child homelessness rates in the nation. And many of those children had parents who were incarcerated, and lived in temporary living situations, like living with friends or family. Child homelessness has an impact on the future of communities as it impacts personal relationships, employment, and the long-term health of the child.[53] Oklahoma State Agencies have also experienced budget shortages in paying for social services, like child welfare and

Medicaid programs that help seniors and people with disabilities.[43] And due to financial constraints, the State made cuts in mental health services to treat people with addictions and mental health problems.

These are not the only negative consequences. As the State of Oklahoma puts more people in prisons, and more people are released at a future date, you have to consider the contribution those people will make once they are released. Will they be more likely to cope with the problems they face, which may include employment discrimination and other forms of discrimination? Will their mental health, self-confidence, and outlook on life improve to the point to where they are stable and independent enough to not reoffend? Or will those people have mental health problems, substance abuse, and unemployment, which could continue to burden communities? It's difficult to see how any of the behavioral problems that lead to incarceration in the first place could improve while incarcerated without some social program capable of developing the life skills that enable people to be independent and responsible adults.

Even the labeling effect can cause problems, especially if the person was convicted of a victimless Misdemeanor crime, and was is labeled a Felon for life because of mandatory sentencing. Even when the person has a perfect record afterword, and receives an advanced level of education, makes all the right choices, and contributes to the greater good, that person remains a Felon. In States, like Oklahoma, that becomes a problem when you have At-Will employment laws that give employers the freedom to hire and fire people for any reason. While some Federal agencies ask applicants if they have received a Felony in the last seven years, the majority of corporate applications in Oklahoma ask if the applicant has ever been convicted of a crime another than a misdemeanor.

Since that time, mostly has a result of severe economic repercussions, Oklahoma has started reforming their laws. They now allow people who committed a crime that is normally considered a misdemeanor, to get their record expunged after a period of time. But even with an expungement, under the current law, they still have to get a pardon to get their rights restored. What that effectively means is that, under Oklahoma law, people who had their record expunged can tell future employers that they have not committed a crime, but do not have full rights as a citizen.

So, even ten or twenty years after the fact, if the person seeks a Pardon for the Felony, that person goes through the same process as a capital offender (i.e., someone who is guilty for a crime, like murder). And that person will likely be denied the pardon. In the case of a misdemeanor offense, that denial would do nothing to keep citizens safer, or warn citizens of a potential danger, or prevent the person from reoffending. It simply subjects the person to greater discrimination and potential difficulty finding employment, and would force the person to live with unnecessary social and financial hardships.

In 2001, Sociology Professor Devah Pager studied the effects of incarceration and how people who were formerly incarcerated have a lower position in firms and make less income. A number of theories exist for this, she says: "the labeling effects of criminal stigma, the disruption of social and family networks, the loss of human capital, institutional trauma, and legal barriers to employment."[49] One problem, according to her research, is that a criminal record attaches a kind of "negative credential" that may qualify a person for exclusion in the employment process.

To observe this, Pager conducted a study with two black, and two white, male college students that were described as "bright and articulate." Together, they audited a total of 350 employers in Milwaukee, Wisconsin, a State where people with a criminal record are protected by law from being discriminated against by employers, unless the offense is relevant to the position. During different weeks, the students were randomly assigned a criminal record of a felony conviction which consisted of "possession of cocaine with intent to distribute." Each applicant applied for a job requiring no more than a high school education. Under their work experience, each put work experience from the correctional facility, and each cited their parole officer as a reference on the application. About 75 percent of the employers asked the applicants about their criminal offenses and for details about those offenses. A little more than 25 percent told the applicant they would perform a background check. Among equally qualified participants, about half as many whites with a criminal record were called back by employers in comparison with those that did not. And only one-third of the blacks with a record were called back.[49]

6

Opportunities for Improvement

Deterring crime by increasing the severity of punishments has proven ineffective because it does nothing to change the underlying causes of social problems, which may include mental disorders, skills deficits, or some other developmental problems. Criminal justice should be fair to people and impose punishments that are proportional to the offender's actions. And Correctional facilities, as their name implies, should try to correct the offender's behavior and prevent the person from reoffending. Offenders of certain types of crimes, like Misdemeanor crimes, theft, drug related crimes, or victimless crimes, stand a much better chance of benefiting from treatment programs than violent offenders. Rehabilitation should try to prepare those people, in terms of mental health and life skills, to transition back into the community.

An arrest is an opportunity to remove an offender from the community to hold the offender accountable and prevent additional harm. But an arrest is also an opportunity to intervene in the offender's behavior, to change the thinking that motivated the criminal offense. Every minute an inmate is in State custody, the State has the opportunity to influence that inmate's behavior. And every minute the State lacks an effective program, government officials throw away that opportunity to make the community safer when those inmates are released.

If State officials are truly working to make communities safer, then they will provide inmates with the treatment programs to improve mental health and develop the life skills necessary to successfully transition back into the community. Without those improvements, you should have no expectation that an inmate's behavior or condition will improve. And those programs need ongoing research to make them more effective overtime. Measures of progress could also be put in place to make sure these programs are, in fact, reducing crime and taxpayer burden, and improving public safety.

# REFERENCES

1. Adler, A. (1949). Understanding Human Nature. (W. B. Wolfe, M.D., Trans.). (pp. 8, 134). New York: Permabooks. (Original work published 1927)
2. All Things Considered. (April 4, 2016). New Orleans Man Faces 20 Years To Life For Candy Bar Theft. Retrieve April 5, 2016 from http://www.npr.org/2016/04/04/473004950/new-orleans-man-faces-20-years-to-life-for-candy-bar-theft
3. American Humane. (n.d.). Emotional Abuse. Retrieved April 8, 2007, from http://www.americanhumane.org
4. American Institute of Stress. (n.d.). Job Stress. Retrieved March 31, 2007, from http://www.stress.org/job.htm
5. American Institute of Stress. (n.d.). Stress, Definition of Stress, Stressor, What is Stress?, Eustress?. Retrieved March 31, 2007, from http://www.stress.org/americas.htm
6. Angwin, J., Larson, J., Mattu, S., Kirchner, L., Machine Bias. ProPublica. Retrieved January 27, 2018 from https://www.propublica.org/article/machine-bias-risk-assessments-in-criminal-sentencing

7. Ansink J. (September 10, 2013). C-suite suicides: When exec life becomes a nightmare. Fortune. Retrieved September 7, 2015 from http://fortune.com/2013/09/10/c-suite-suicides-when-exec-life-becomes-a-nightmare

8. Baker, M. (August 27, 2015). Over half of psychology studies fail reproducibility test. Nature.com. Retrieved November 25, 2017 from https://www.nature.com/news/over-half-of-psychology-studies-fail-reproducibility-test-1.18248

9. Cannon, W. B. (1963). Bodily Changes in Pain, Hunger, Fear and Rage. (2nd ed., pp. 195, 243-244). New York: Harper Torchbooks. (Original work published 1920)

10. Centers for Disease Control and Prevention (CDC). (2006, May 2). Fetal Alcohol Information. Retrieved April 8, 2007, from http://www.cdc.gov/ncbddd/fas/fasask.htm

11. Corbin, C. B., Corbin, W. R., Welk, G. J., & Welk, K.A. (2006). Concepts of Fitness and Wellness: A Comprehensive Lifestyle Approach (6th ed., p. 295). University of Central Oklahoma. Boston: McGraw-Hill Custom Publishing

12. Dalio, R. (September 19, 2017). Principles: Life and Work. Simon & Schuster.

13. Department of Health and Human Services. (2000, November). Healthy People 2010: Under-standing and Improving Health (2nd ed), pp. 9-3, 9-5, 9-6. Washington, DC: U.S. Government Printing Office

14. Department of Health and Human Services. (2000, November). Healthy People 2010: Under-standing and Improving Health (2nd ed), pp. 16-3, 16-4, 16-5. Washington, DC: U.S. Government Printing Office

15. Department of Health and Human Services. (2000, November). Healthy People 2010: Understanding and Improving Health (2nd ed), pp. 18-3 – 18-5, 18-15, 18-19, 18-20, 18-26. Washington, DC: U.S. Government Printing Office

16. Department of Health and Human Services. (2000, November). Healthy People 2010: Understanding and Improving Health (2nd ed), p. 26-3. Washington, DC: U.S. Government Printing Office.

17. Duhigg, C. (February 25, 2016). What Google Learned From Its Quest to Build the Perfect Team. The New York Times. Retrieved April 17, 2016 from http://www.nytimes.com/2016/02/28/magazine/what-google-learned-from-its-quest-to-build-the-perfect-team.html.

18. Duhigg, C. (February 28, 2012). The Power of Habit: Why We Do What We Do in Life and Business. Random House.

19. Durkheim, Emile. Moral Education. Trans. Everett K Wilson, Herman Schnurer. New York: The Free Press of Glencoe, 1961. p. 121

20. Dweck, C. (February 28, 2006). Mindset: The New Psychology of Success. Random House; 1 edition.

21. eMedicineHealth. (2005, August 10). Substance Abuse. Retrieved March 31, 2007, from http://www.emedicinehealth.com/substance_abuse/article_em.htm

22. Ericsson, A. (April 11, 20017). Peak: Secrets from the New Science of Expertise. Eamon Dolan Books Paper.

23. Felder, B. (May 17, 2017). NewsOK. Oklahoma school districts move on cuts without clear budget

picture. Retrieve August 26, 2017 from http://new-sok.com/article/5549452.

24. Freud, S. (1950). Totem and Taboo. (J. Strachey, Trans.). (Standard ed., p. 63). New York: Norton. (Original work published 1913)

25. Fromm, E. (1990). The Sane Society. (p. 65). New York: Owl Books. (Original work published 1955)

26. Haas, P. (November 4, 2017). The Real Reason to be Afraid of Artificial Intelligence. TEDxDirigo. Retrieved January 27, 2018 from https://www.tedxdirigo.com/talks/the-real-reason-to-be-afraid-of-artificial-intelligence

27. Heathfield, S. (October 11, 2017). The 2 Most Important Management Secrets: Pygmalion and Galatea Effects. The Balance. Retrieved December 17, 2017 from https://www.thebalance.com/pygmalion-and-galatea-effects-1918677

28. Hock, Roger R. (2002). Forty Studies that Changed Psychology: Explorations into the History of Psychological Research. 4th ed. Upper Saddle River, New Jersey: Prentice Hall.

29. Hock, Roger R. (2002). Forty Studies that Changed Psychology: Explorations into the History of Psychological Research. 4th ed. (pp. 71-72). Upper Saddle River, New Jersey: Prentice Hall.

30. Innocence Project. (n.d.). False Confessions or Admissions. Retrieved September 2, 2016 from http://www.innocenceproject.org/causes/false-confessions-admissions

31. Investopedia. (n.d.). Gambler's Fallacy. Retrieved March 19, 2016 from http://www.investopedia.com/terms/g/gamblersfallacy.asp

32. Kahneman, D. (2011). Thinking Fast and Slow. Farrar, Straus and Giroux. New York. Chapter 10.

33. Konnikova, M. (November 18, 2013). On the Face of It: The Psychology of Electability. The New Yorker. Retrieved April 17, 2016, from http://www.newyorker.com/tech/elements/on-the-face-of-it-the-psychology-of-electability

34. Landau, E. (February 10, 2009). Study: Experiences make us happier than possessions. CNN. Retrieved April 23, 2016 from http://www.cnn.com/2009/HEALTH/02/10/happiness.possessions

35. Livingston, S. (January 2003). Pygmalion in Management. Harvard Business Review. Retrieved on December 17, 2017 from https://hbr.org/2003/01/pygmalion-in-management.

36. Llopis, G. (October 21, 2017). Unconscious Bias Training Perpetuates The Problems America Strives To Fix. Forbes. Retrived May 26, 2018 from https://www.forbes.com/sites/glennllopis/2017/10/21/unconscious-bias-training-perpetuates-the-problems-america-strives-to-fix

37. Loftus, E. F. (1975). Leading questions and the eyewitness report. Cognitive Psychology, 7(4), 560-572.

38. Machiavelli, N. (1966). The Prince. (D. Donno, Trans.). (p. 70). New York: Bantam Dell. (Original work published 1532)

39. Mankiewicz, Josh. (June 7, 2019). She did everything right. Nbcnews.com Retrieved June 13, 2019, from https://www.nbcnews.com/dateline/video/dateline-monday-preview-she-did-everything-right-61485125594

40. March of Dimes Foundation. (2006, April). Birth Defects. Retrieved April 8, 2007, from http://www.marchofdimes.com/professionals/14332_1206.asp
41. Maslow, A. H. (1976). The Farther Reaches of Human Nature. (pp. 26, 117). New York: Penguin.
42. Mayo Clinic. (2006, June 26). Tips for Coping with Stress. Retrieved March 30, 2007, from http://www.mayoclinic.com/health/coping-with-stress
43. McCleland, J. (January 10, 2017). KGOU. Oklahoma Department Of Human Services Requests Supplemental Funding. Retrieved August 26, 2017 from http://kgou.org/post/oklahoma-department-human-services-requests-supplemental-funding
44. Morse, G. (January 2006). Decisions and Desire. The Harvard Business Review. Retrieved August 4, 2018, from https://hbr.org/2006/01/decisions-and-desire
45. National Center for Injury Prevention and Control. (2006, September 7). Suicide: Fact Sheet. Retrieved March 31, 2007, from http://www.cdc.gov/ncipc/factsheets/suifacts.htm
46. National Institute of Mental Health (NIMH). (2006, September 13). Depression. Retrieved March 31, 2007, from http://www.nimh.nih.gov/publicat/depression.cfm
47. National Institute of Mental Health (NIMH). (2007, January 24). Schizophrenia. Retrieved March 31, 2007, from http://www.nimh.nih.gov/publicat/schizoph.cfm
48. OSSBA. Oklahoma's Teacher Shortage Deepens: District Leaders Describe Mixed Experiences with

Emergency Certified Teachers. Retrieved August 26, 2017 from https://www.ossba.org/2017/08/22/oklahomas-teacher-shortage-deepens.

49. Pager, D. (2004). The Mark of a Criminal Record. Focus (Vol. 23, No. 2), p. 44. Retrieved April 7, 2007, from http://www.irp.wisc.edu/publications/focus/pdfs/foc232i.pdf

50. Pew Research Center. (October 30, 2014). People in Emerging Markets Catch Up to Advanced Economies in Life Satisfaction: Asians Most Optimistic about Future, Middle Easterners the Least. Retrieved April 3, 2016 from http://www.pewglobal.org/2014/10/30/people-in-emerging-markets-catch-up-to-advanced-economies-in-life-satisfaction

51. Pink, D. (April 5, 2011). Drive: The Surprising Truth About What Motivates Us. Riverhead Books.

52. Reed, W. & Schanzenbach, M. (1996). Chapter 27: OSHA - We're From the Government and We're Here to Help You. Prices and Information: A Simple Framework for Understanding Economics. Retrieved April 1, 2007, from http://www.ou.edu/class/econ3003/book/area1c27.html

53. Robson, N. (November 23, 2014). Oklahoma Watch: Number of homeless children in Oklahoma is among highest in nation. NewOK.com. Retrieved July 6, 2017 from http://newsok.com/article/5369190

54. Seligman, M., Stillwell, K. (April 3, 2018). The Hope Circuit: A Psychologist's Journey from Helplessness to Optimism. PublicAffairs.

55. Skinner, B. F. (1976). About Behaviorism. (p. 64). New York: Vintage.
56. Thaler, R., Sunstein, C. (February 24, 2009). Nudge: Improving Decisions About Health, Wealth, and Happiness. Penguin Books.
57. The Muse. (March 19, 2013). The Secret to Motivating Your Team. Forbes. Retrieve April 16, 2016 from http://www.forbes.com/sites/dailymuse/2013/03/19/the-secret-to-motivating-your-team/#597d4255433f
58. Turner, C. (MARCH 11, 2015). The Teenage Brain: Spock Vs. Captain Kirk. Retrieved March 12, 2015, from http://www.npr.org/blogs/ed/2015/03/11/391864852/the-teenage-brain-spock-vs-captain-kirk
59. Umberson, D., Montez, J. K. (2010) Social Relationships and Health: A Flashpoint for Health Policy. Journal of Health and Social Behavior. Retrieved September 7, 2015 from http://hsb.sagepub.com/content/51/1_suppl/S54.full.pdf
60. Visser, S. (June 12, 2016). Euro 2016: Dozens injured as crowds of rival fans brawl. CNN. Retrieved June 12, 2016 from http://www.cnn.com/2016/06/11/world/euro-2016-england-russia-brawl
61. Volkow, N. D., Koob, G. F., & McLellan, A. T. (January 28, 2016). Neurobiologic Advances from the Brain Disease Model of Addiction. The New England Journal of Medicine. Retrieved January 30, 2016 from http://www.nejm.org/doi/full/10.1056/NEJMra1511480

62. Watson, J. B., & Rayner, R. (1920). Conditioned emotional responses. Journal of Experimental Psychology, 3.

# INDEX

65244354R00135

Made in the USA
Middletown, DE
02 September 2019